Foreword

We are aware of the significant changes, yet it is difficult to place absolutely what has changed and what is evolving. We are uncertain about the future. There are changes in the conventional methods of getting things done. New advancements or cycles in innovation, computational thinking, design thinking, web-based media, virtual reality, augmented reality, artificial intelligence, data analytics and other emerging fields are changing each feature of the human experience. Ground-breaking new advancements are globalizing pretty much every part of the present world, and this disturbance holds tremendous ramifications for our networks, families, and the eventual fate of instructing and learning. What does the future hold for us? What are the disruptions in teaching and learning? What are the future jobs? What are the skill sets required? What are the emerging tools and technology?

The impressive change can be found in the lives of youngsters who convey, mingle and partake online easily. Students are progressively grasping innovation at a more youthful age … yet the study halls of today don't mirror these changes. While there has been interest in innovation at universities, it has unquestionably not changed how instruction is conveyed. Change of any sort is difficult to accept for the human condition. Individuals love the familiar, the regular, the normal and the everyday practice. Here and there for individuals, the absence of progress turns into the familiar object that keeps up a fixed attitude and unsurprising world. Unfortunately, the teachers and educators didn't get this message!

The EduTech and Skill Tech team of Centurion University of Technology and Management responds to this call to innovation and disruption. The book 'Education Technology for Engagement and Experience' contains thirteen chapters in the areas of education technology, engagement and experience. Commencing with the Flipped Class: Creating Value in Education, it goes over to Learning in the Virtual Space: Challenges and Opportunities, COVID-19 Prediction Using ARIMA Model, Object Detection and Analysis Using Amazon recognition, Silly Mistakes in Regression Analysis, "Utopia" The Immersive Reality, Need of Machine Learning in Smart Agriculture, Impartus: Integrating Multiple Strategies for Improving Reading Skills, Mind Mapping: A Powerful Tool for Visual Thinking and Learning, Technology-oriented Learning and its Tools: Open Broadcaster Software, Virtual Learning and Confidence Building in Public Space, Virtualization Framework for Big Data Application and Adobe Spark: An Aid to Online Teaching Platform. This book is comprehensively written for students across all disciplines, teachers and educators. The main purpose is to gain a better understanding of the effectiveness of such recent tools and technology in achieving the learning outcomes, explore how immersive experiences can further amplify learner's ability to understand complex concepts and help educational organisations to prepare for uncertainties. The book chapters are a reflection of the current practices at Centurion University of Technology and Management.

Table of Contents

MIND MAPPING: A POWERFUL TOOL FOR VISUAL THINKING AND LEARNING

Dr. Prajna Pani
Professor
Centurion University of Technology and Management
Odisha, India

INTRODUCTION

In this age of discontinuities and disruption, there is a need to see challenges and opportunities to help teachers, instructional designers, educators and policy makers to lead through transformational leadership. Visual thinking meets these needs by promoting creativity, calling for collaboration and sharing of ideas, and above all, making learning visible. Visual thinking is a game-changing practice that complements to the design thinking process. The endeavour is to integrate insights from three areas: (1) Literature Review, (2) Mind Mapping Software and Tools and (3) Pedagogical Practices. The purpose is to introduce visual thinking as a culture in this chapter. Powerful visual communication tools such as MindMup, Coogle, Mindmeister can be embedded in the curriculum to facilitate for a rich meaningful learning journey that incorporates questioning, deep thinking, collaborating, brainstorming and understanding. This chapter provides a window to see the evidences of how it can be incorporated in the IELTS (International English Language Testing System) Class.

MIND MAPPING AND VISUAL THINKING

Visual thinking is an indispensable expertise for growing novel thoughts and plans, imparting those thoughts viably, and working together with others to make them genuine. Visual thinking is a game-changing practice that invigorates groups, supports inventiveness, and gives more prominent lucidity into objectives, ventures and plans. Visual thinking is presented as a culture in this part. It is an astounding supplement to the plan thinking draws near. Mind mapping in instruction is a drawing in strategy for meaningful learning.

Mind maps go under an assortment of names. When all is said in done, they are known as semantic planning, idea maps, think-joins, realistic coordinators, information planning, or psychological guides. As John Dewey and different researchers state, students have various capacities, intellectual spaces, learning styles, and shifting degrees of insight in various territories, including visual knowledge. The training system without anyone else doesn't really bring about an important learning experience. All together for an important figuring out how to happen, students ought to relate and connect new information with applicable subjects that they definitely know, all in all, outwardly arrange data, thoughts, and contemplations for better getting, recollecting, and reviewing of material.

Visual Thinking School energizes cooperation through a gathering critical thinking measure. It utilizes craftsmanship to show thinking, relational abilities, and visual education. Visual thinking is a strategy that utilizations instruments to externalize inward reasoning cycles, making them more understood, unequivocal, and significant. Visual thinking causes you sort out your musings and improve your capacity to think and convey. It's additionally an incredible method to pass on complex or possibly befuddling data. Mind mapping causes us to extend our intuition past our standard ideal models. It can assist you with seeing the catch complex thoughts rapidly and effectively and distinguish connections among thoughts and cycles.

As a learning tool, concept maps were first introduced by Novak and his colleagues in Cornell University in the 70s of last century. Concept maps are based on Asubel's theory of meaningful learning which states that "learning is meaningful when the student comprehends the relationship of what is being learned to other knowledge" (KILIÇ & ÇAKMAK, 2013).

Mind map is one of the best techniques for discovering that utilizations conceptualizing from an information idea to a connected branch. Instructors can screen and advance students' learning and thoroughly considering the utilization of idea mind map. Idea guides could be depicted as a visual method of speaking to information in which ideas, connections and recommendations exist. One of the significant troubles that students face in article composing is basically absence of important plans to compose their exposition convincingly till the end. In this way, they battle with uncertainties about their composing capacities and become unsure about communicating. Given this, it is truly fascinating that applying the idea of idea planning can surprisingly quicken the inclination for learning new snippets of data unquestionably more rapidly and effectively than previously and quicken the cycle of exposition composing. Mind-planning is viewed as an amazing asset to assist students with problems and issues with the association of their thoughts and contemplations.

This chapter begins with thought-provoking questions that you can use to explore where you stand as a visual thinker:

1. In the last month, have you drawn a diagram to explain something to someone?
2. Do you use drawn diagrams/mind maps to help yourself understand or remember information?
3. Have you visited different websites in the last 6 months to design your thinking and solve problems?
4. Do you to take notes using mind maps?
5. Do you use mind maps to brainstorm and solve problems?
6. Can you visualize what an education landscape might be like by after a year?
7. Do you enjoy editing your digital photographs to improve?

8. Do you use 3D images in teaching and learning to give better experience to your students?

OBJECTIVES

The aim is to find methods suitable for IELTS teaching and learning that would achieve the following

- Student involvement and collaboration

- Improve student comprehension and performance

- Express ideas visually and creatively

- Encourages self-reflection

- Stimulates interest in IELTS teaching and learning

The instructional techniques provide a meaningful context and platform for IELTS practice. Some of the best methods to teach IELTS are:

- Collaborative activities to develop language proficiency

- Hands-on activities which encourage unconscious learning of language

- Brainstorming

MIND MAPPING SOFTWARE AND TOOLS

Classroom lessons can be designed using Mind Map tools such as MindMeister, Mindomo, MindMup, Coggle FreeMind and embedded in the curriculum to facilitate for a rich meaningful learning journey that incorporates questioning, deep thinking, brainstorming and understanding. This chapter uses the four skills -Listening, Speaking, Reading and Writing (IELTS) to explain how visual thinking can be implemented in the English course and inspires course design and delivery.

TABLE-1: Comparison Table of Mind Mapping Software

MINDMAP TOOLS	USES
Mind Master	Mind mapping, brainstorming, presentation, project management, team collaboration
Mind Mup	Convert maps easily to PDF, PowerPoint & outlines Publish and share maps online. Easily save to Google Drive and manage using Google Apps.
Mindomo	For concept mapping and education
FreeMind	Maps, Charts, Diagrams
MindManager	Maps, Charts, Diagrams
Lucid Chart	Flowcharts, process maps
Bubbl.us	Mapping, Outlining, Big Data Presenting
MindMup	Mind maps
Coggle	Flowcharts, Process maps & other diagrams
XMind 8	Mind mapping Business Charts
Creately	Flowcharts, UML, Mockups
MindGenius	Mind mapping, Project management, Brainstorming

MIND MAPPING IN EDUCATION

Mind mapping is a powerful skill in the field of education. Students can use mind map tools to acquire grammatical knowledge and gain word power, brainstorm for essay writing and story writing; summarize text, take notes from lectures, talks; collaborate with teams to work on projects. Teachers can use mind map tools to visualize complex information and bring clarity in the concept. Mind maps are a must-have tool in every teacher's repertoire that will make their content more engaging and memorable.

This chapter uses the four skills -Listening, Speaking, Reading and Writing (IELTS) to explain how visual thinking can be implemented in the English course and inspires course design and learning.

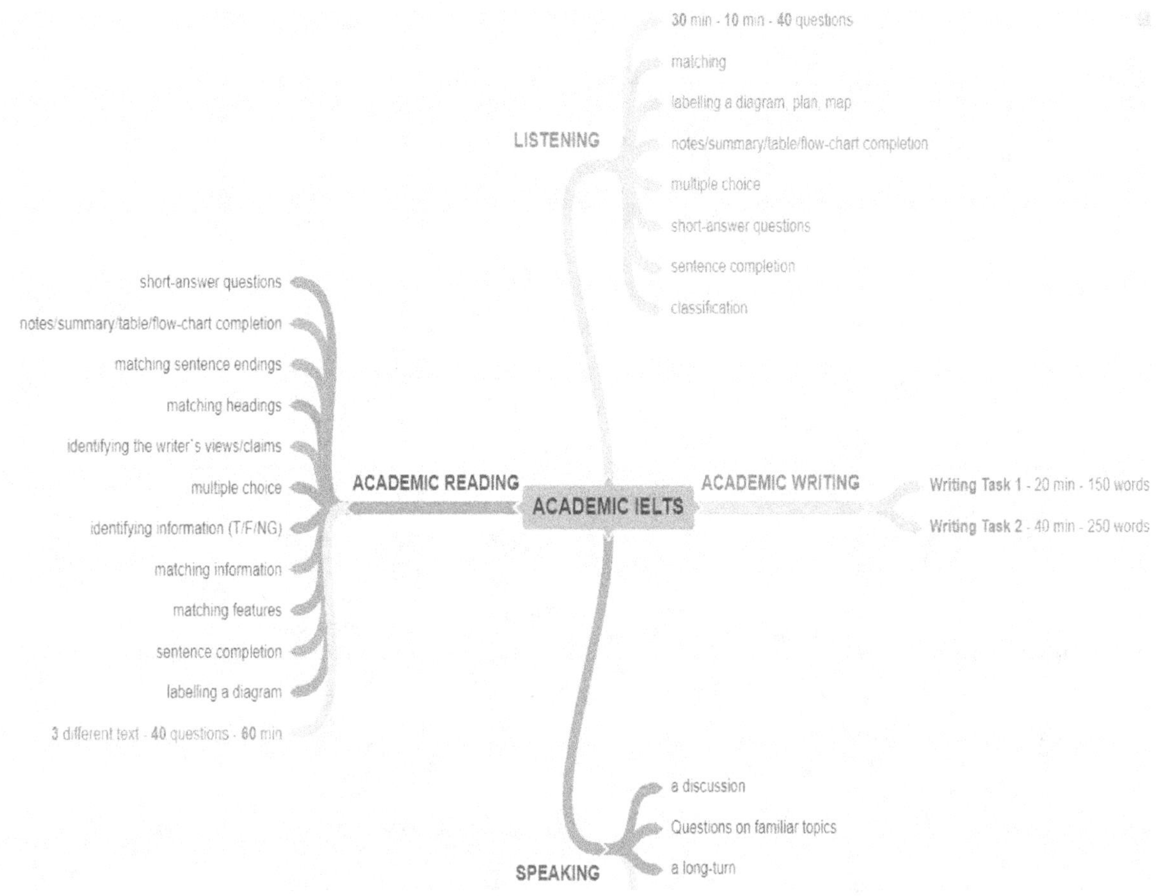

FIGURE 1- IELTS Academic Design

IELTS Listening

People tend to speak fast and fluently so it is difficult to grasp what they say. Words come together in a sentence and, therefore, it is difficult to know if it is an unknown word or a correct expression when listening to it. The pronunciation of words changes in

English, so you must train and practice to understand when listening. A mind map can be prepared on how to improve our listening: (1) Listen and then practice the words that you think are hard to understand when they say them, (2) Through videos in English you can try to understand and know a little better the pronunciation, (3) There are videos that explain how certain words are pronounced, (4) Watching movies, series and more in English helps improve your vocabulary and listening.

Learners can listen and re-listen at different speeds, practice more by listening podcasts, TED Talks listen actively by taking notes and be patient. TED Talks for autonomous listening are presented in the mind map.

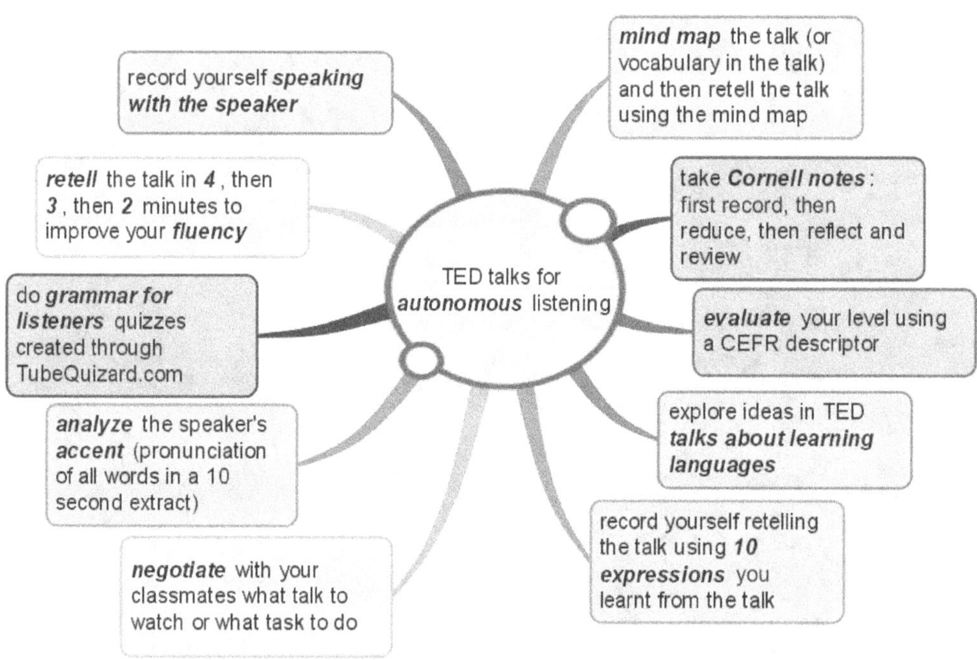

FIGURE 2- Autonomous Learning

IELTS Speaking

Mind Mapping is a visual, brainstorming and pedagogical tool. It can be used for a variety of activities such as planning, organizing and delivering a presentation. Mind maps are powerful ways to visually organize the ideas. A mind map can be useful for IELTS speaking where learners can ask wh-questions such as 'why', 'when', 'who', 'where' etc around the central idea. This will stimulate thinking and generate a response.

Sometimes students find it difficult to arrange/find out ideas for speaking, especially in part 2 when a cue card is given and the candidate is asked to speak. Hopefully the mind-map on fear of public speaking and similar brainstorming on other topics will help the students to speak on a topic card or more complex questions for sometime. The visual representation of the nuggets to neutralize the fear of public speaking is shown in Figure 3.

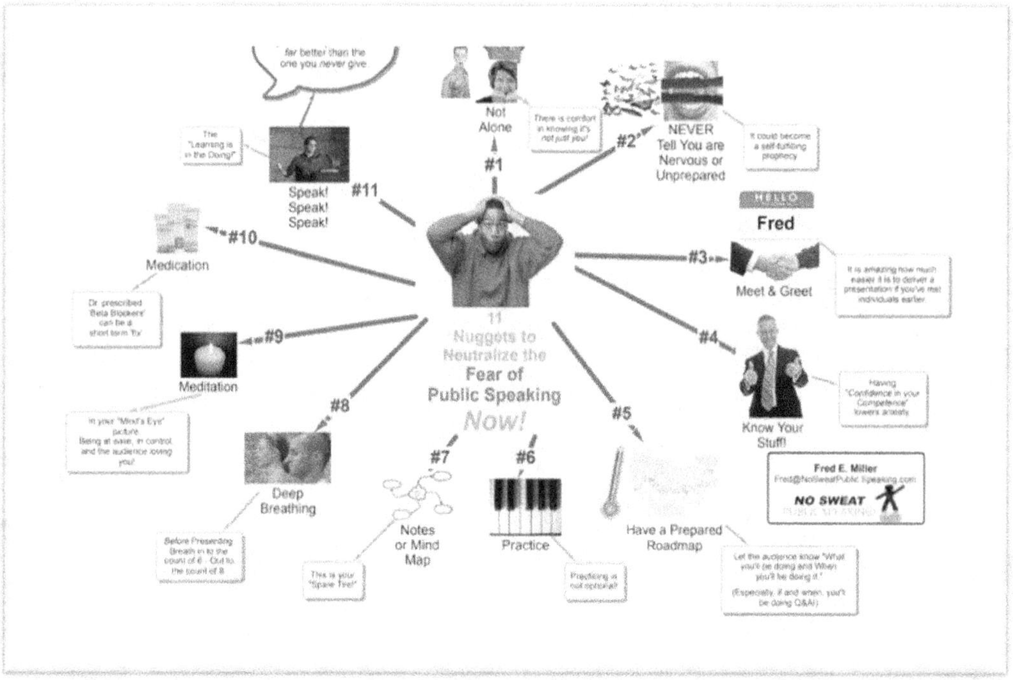

FIGURE 3 - Fear of Public Speaking (2013) Adapted from <https://nosweatpublicspeaking.com>

IELTS Reading

Students can use a mind map to draw the central idea of an article. Another great exercise is using Mind Maps to learn vocabulary. Using mind maps, students can focus on technical vocabulary pertinent to the science class, without having to consider complex sentence structure and grammar (Harper & Jong, 2004). Mindmeister tool is used the reading comprehension tools such as Applications, Digital Books/eReaders Functions, and analyses effective reading strategies.

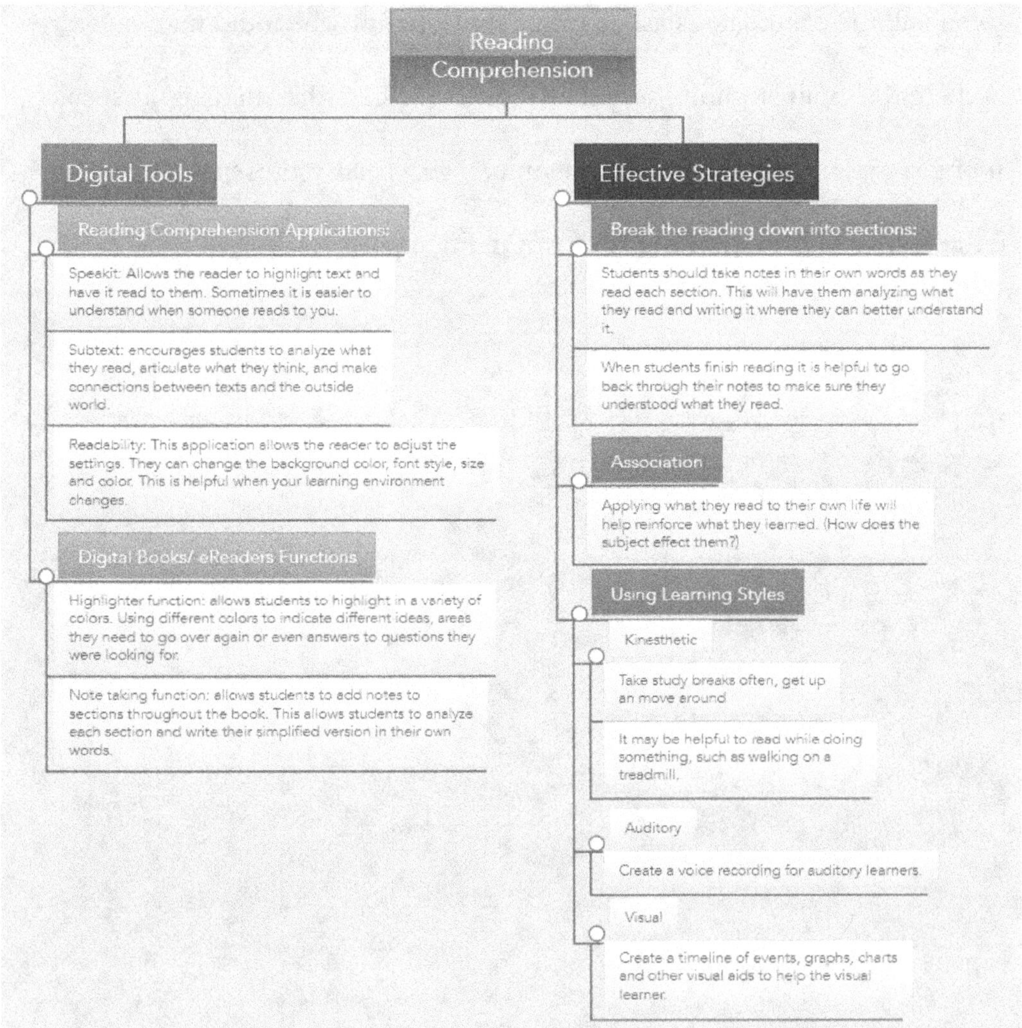

FIGURE 4- Reading comprehension (Mindmeister)

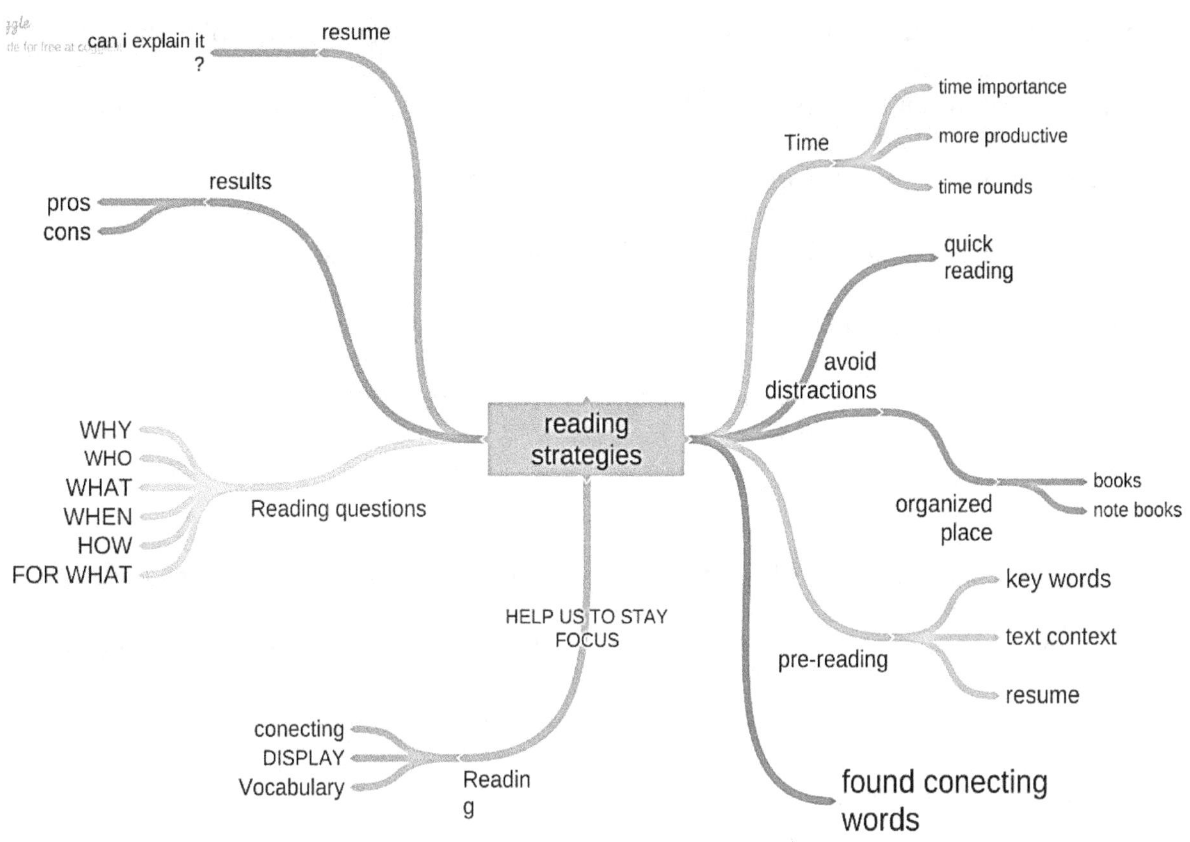

FIGURE 5 - Reading Strategies

IELTS Writing

The heart of teaching and learning of higher education revolves round scholar writing skills. A huge variety of strategies is determined to be evolved for coaching essay writing in diverse geographical contexts for different political, ancient and social reasons. In the remaining decades, using feedback in English appears to be stronger as a second/ overseas language (ESL/EFL) writing instruction. Online mind mapping starts from an idea. MindMeister is an online mind mapping application that allows learners to visualize, share and present thoughts and ideas via the cloud. MindMeister can be used to make online plans, make efficient notes and collaborate, visual brainstorming for teams and manage team's collective intelligence. It can be efficiently used for note taking, pros and cons, meeting minutes, lesson plan, class

13

syllabus and exam preparation. The mind mapping strategy may be used to explore a good vary of topics in writing and conjointly utilized in all types of writing such as: narrative, descriptive, recount, persuasive and argumentative. A recent study demonstrates that students who may express their learning with visual skills had a 40% higher retention rate than that of just verbal learners (Adam & Mowers, 2007). This shows the potential importance of this method in writing classes, and it looks it's a helpful strategy to support students throughout writing tasks.

Most of the students are not aware about the brainstorming method which is a pre-writing process where one is induced to think about the given topic and present the idea through a mind map. It will further guide to write and proceed. For example, a student can draw a mind map on the questions 'What is my goal? How will I achieve it'. The sub-topics could be search jobs, prepare for jobs, sign up for value added and trending courses, learn a new language, get contact information, attend training classes, work on industry-integrated projects and get a better job.

Students can use Cornell method to take notes and summarise.

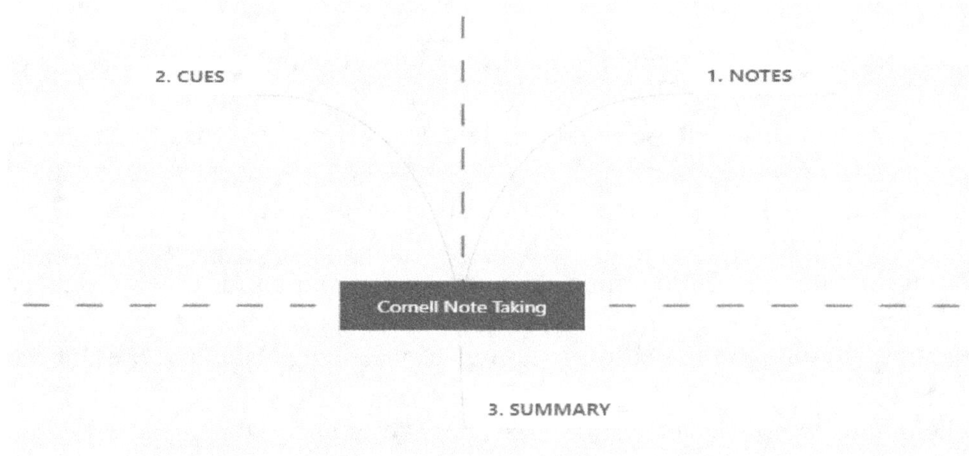

FIGURE 6 - Cornell Note Taking

Teachers can use the "Essay Structure" template under "education" category to teach the students how to organize an essay with introduction, body and conclusion. For, example an essay can include supporting facts, argument, rationale, opposing arguments and conclusion.

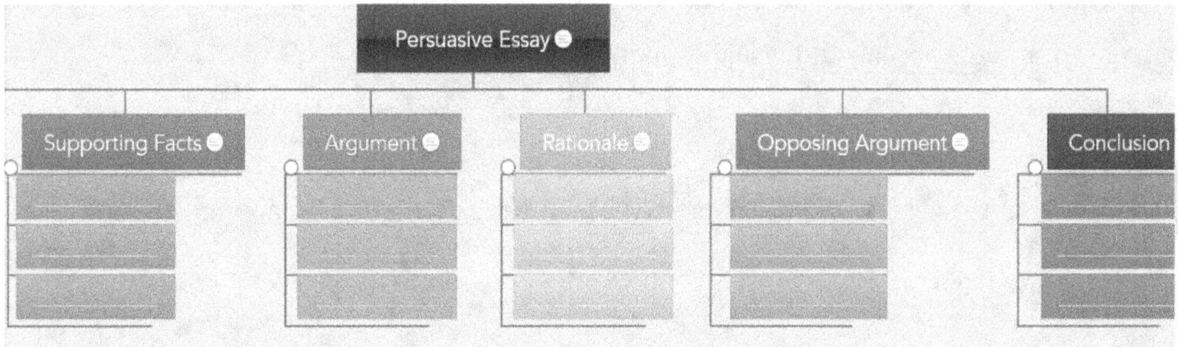

FIGURE 7- Essay Structure

This chapter showcases how an essay on the strategies for climate change can be developed using a mind mapping method.

FIGURE 8- Example of mind map on essay writing strategies (The University of Adelaide, 2014)

CONCLUSION

This chapter explored numerous brainstorming approaches in LSRW activities. Literature review shows that brainstorming and mind mapping are engaging tools for that can help teachers, facilitators, and learners to overcome the challenges in listening, speaking, reading and writing and make it more fun. Hence, this technique should be adopted and embedded in IELTS courses. The paper also highlights a paradigm shift in teaching and learning to a new innovative one that involves adaption of technology in IELTS activities. However, more analysis is required to substantiate the effectiveness of mind map tools and gain insight into the advantages of mind mapping and visual thinking.

REFERENCES

1. Adam, A., & Mowers, H. (2007). Get inside their heads with mind mapping. School library journal, 53(3), 24.

2. Gray, Dave. Adapted from <http://www.xplaner.com/>

3. Mind Mapping (2014).Writing Centre Learning Guide, The University of Adelaide. http://www.greendealsolutions.net/wp-content/uploads/2013/03/strategies-for-change.jpg

4. Mustafa KILIÇ and Murset ÇAKMAK (2013). Concept maps as a tool for meaningful learning and teaching in chemistry education (research paper).

5. Reading comprehension (Mindmeister). Taken from <https://www.mindmeister.com/556835017/reading comprehension>

6. Svantesson, I. (1989). Mind mapping & memory: Powerful techniques to help you make better use of your brain. London: Kogan Page.

7. Teaching, Academy for Teaching and Learning Excellence. Adapted from https://www.usf.edu/atle/teaching/visual-thinking strategies

8. Yolanda Iglesias, Visual thinking. Adapted from <https://designthinking.gal/en/visual-thinking/

FLIPPED CLASSROOM:
CREATING VALUE IN EDUCATION

Ms. Kalapoorna Nalla
Research Scholar
Centurion University of Technology and Management
Odisha, India

INTRODUCTION

The age of disruption and the technological revolution has given a scope for a number of innovations, taking into consideration that the millennial students prefer pedagogical approaches which are interactive and collaborative and give an experiential learning experience. The flipped classroom is one such pedagogical model which engages the new generation of students in a value-added instructional approach of learning, involving them in active learning techniques. Though this model has been there for some time in the educational field, it has gained an impetus in these disruptive times.

The face-to-face lecture and the didactic approach of teaching is way common in the classrooms. This traditional method of teaching in higher classes and in higher education needs to be revamped to understand the way the students learn in the present times. In comparison to the traditional method students find learning to be more effective and long lasting when they learn with more hands-on activities which comes through collaboration and peer discussion guided by the teacher. As the focus shifts from the teacher to the learner in the changing times, it has become obvious that there needs to be a change in the strategy of teaching so that learning becomes more impactful.

Toady's classrooms are having the millennials. The millennials have been born with technology all around them. They have stepped into this world where they find that technology is all pervading and ubiquitous. Hence, this generation has amassed a lot of attention for the way they behave and their unique characteristics, which are quite different from the previous generation. It is required that the educators understand the new generation of learners so as to be more effective in their approaches toward educating them.

Research suggests that millennial students have a preference for interactive and experiential learning approaches. Flipping the classroom has become an increasingly popular approach to meet the learning needs of present generation students. The flipped-classroom approach to educate the millennial generation is interesting to understand the students' attitudes toward this emerging pedagogy.

This chapter analyses the pros and cons of this interesting approach and the attitudes of the learner and the teacher towards it.

OBJECTIVES

The objectives of this book chapter are:

1. To analyse the pros and cons of flipped classroom
2. To analyse the attitude of the learners and the teachers towards this approach of flipped classroom

LITERATURE REVIEW

Flipped Classroom approach improves the quality of the time in a period where there is a lot of interaction among the students and between the teacher and the students. The responsibility shifts from the teacher to the students. The students become more accountable for their learning. This special type of blended learning engages students in active learning.

There are many definitions of flipped classroom.

- A student-centred method having interactive learning activities in class and the individual teaching platform on computer at home is a flipped classroom (Bishop & Verleger, 2013).

- It is a model that allows students to prepare themselves for the lesson through videos, audios and reading material (Mull, 2012).

- It is an approach that aims at the efficiency of the learning by transferring the knowledge to the students by videos and podcasts and have productive discussions, activities and applications during the class (Milman, 2012).

- As defined by Hamdan (2013), a flipped classroom is not a defined model. It is a model defined by the needs and demands of the students, where teachers use various equipment.

- An opportunity where the students can use their knowledge and can engage in active learning is a flipped classroom (Toto & Nyugen, 2009).

This new approach finds emphasis in the fact that it can be used with different learning methods (Flipped Learning Network-FLN, 2014). The key leaders and the governing body of the Flipped Learning Network (2014) announced a formal definition of the term, so as to bring a clarity into the concept of 'flipped learning'. It defines flipped learning as a pedagogical approach in which direct instruction moves from the group learning space to the individual learning space, and the resulting group space is transformed into a dynamic, interactive learning environment where the educator guides students as they apply concepts and engage creatively in the subject matter. Prince (2004) enumerates significant evidence of the benefits of active learning, which is the backbone of a flipped classroom. Active learning requires the students to think and reflect on what they have done through meaningful activities. Baeten et al. (2010) discover that approaches that are student-centred, among other factors, direct the learning of the students to a deep approach by the students.

It has been seen that in different disciplines of study, the approach to traditional method of teaching has been received with less interest and enthusiasm by the students. The medical students find the interactive approaches to be more effective than the didactic lectures which they perceive as a least effective as a learning tool (Butler, 1992). Students of Biology significantly improved their performance in the assessments when active learning was introduced where students did problem solving in groups through discussions and collaboration (Armbruster et al., 2009). The key determinants in student performance are active participation in discussions and hands on activities in small groups and the feedback given on these activities by the teachers (Garfield, 1995). It has been noted that students who are in first year studying medicine, business and psychology disciplines expect to be taught in the traditional formal method but prefer to learn in an interactive and group-based activities method (Sander et al., 2009). First year Statistics students improved their performance when they started "doing statistics" in their course (Smith, 1998). Courses need to be aligned constructively so that the desired learning outcomes are realized through the activities required to be done by the students and the teaching-learning methodology with the formative and summative assessments are consistent defining the learning outcomes (Biggs & Tang, 2000). The "inverted classroom" (Lage et al., 2000) or the "flipped-classroom" approach (Baker, 2000), brings active student engagement through problem solving, case studies, etc. by collaborating with their peers, thus focusing the teaching on what the student does actively.

FLIPPED CLASSROOM APPROACH

When preparing a flipped classroom, a teacher needs to comprehend the four pillars of the approach: flexible environment, learning culture, intentional content and professional educator (Bauer et al., 2016).

1. **Flexible environment** indicates an environment which is flexible in time and space for the learner. The students are given a prior exposure to content in the form of videos, audios, presentations, text, notes, etc. This gives the flexibility to the students to be a learner at his/her own pace and also the opportunity to get through the content as many times as he/she requires to understand.

2. **Learning culture** indicates that there has been a shift in the approach to learning from being teacher-centred to student-centred. This transition gives an opportunity to the students to prepare for class through pre assigned quizzes, online discussions and activities.

3. **Intentional content** builds the cognitive skills of a student. The content gives the scope to the students to comprehend at their level and make their own notes. Through this process the learners frame their questions and note down their doubts which are dealt with in the classroom through discussions and activities.

4. **Professional Educator** has a key role in designing qualitative videos, notes and material. The in-class activities that focuses on the development of the higher level cognitive skills are facilitated and also evaluated. A feedback is provided to the students. The active learning by means of discussions, activities, peer-learning, problem-solving and case studies accommodates the deep learning of the learner.

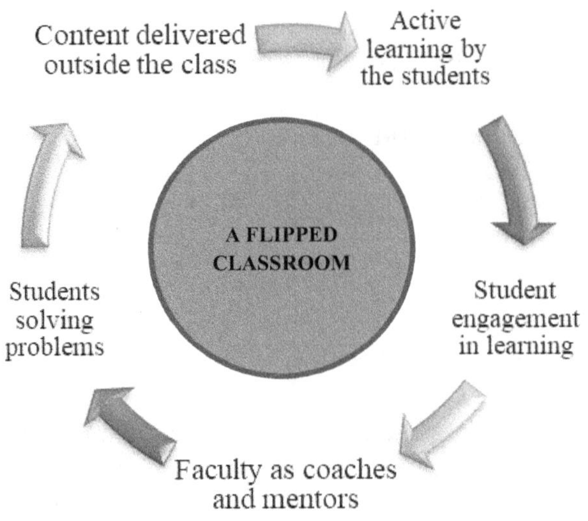

FIGURE 1: A Model of a Flipped Classroom

Since flipped classroom approach/flipped learning has a theoretical base, it accounts for the success and popularity among the learners. The basic elements of learning, transmission of knowledge or information, is conducted independently by the students outside the classroom. Through analysis, synthesis and critical thinking, this information is assimilated in the classrooms under the capable guidance of the teacher. This method finds a sync with the Bloom's Taxonomy. The problem-solving tasks assigned to the students in a flipped classroom ask the students to utilise the prior given information by constructing their knowledge through experiences, interaction and reflection. Thus, constructivism theory finds relevance in a flipped classroom. Implementing flipped classroom approach can be time consuming as it requires a lot of careful and curated planning. The videos and audios, notes, materials need to be well selected and administered. Keeping the attention span of the learners in mind, recorded videos or curated videos should not be more than twenty minutes in length. These lectures are not to be repeated in class. In class the time is to be purely devoted to learning in active and a collaborative manner. Digital lectures can be created using Camtasia, Adobe Captivate, Doodly, Adobe Spark, Jing and others, accompanied by digital presentations, Excel spreadsheets, YouTube videos and other relevant materials. The professional educator through observation and analysis gives relevant feedback using pedagogical strategies on the in-class activities and also gets an insight into the individual learning of the students which helps him/her consequently to prepare accordingly for the next class. A debriefing at the end of the class would help the students to understand how the assignment was done and what were the problems faced. A flipped classroom model encourages student-teacher understanding, co-operation and collaboration among students inducing and motivating active learning.

A suggested structure of a seventy-five minutes class (Frydenberg, 2012) can be used.

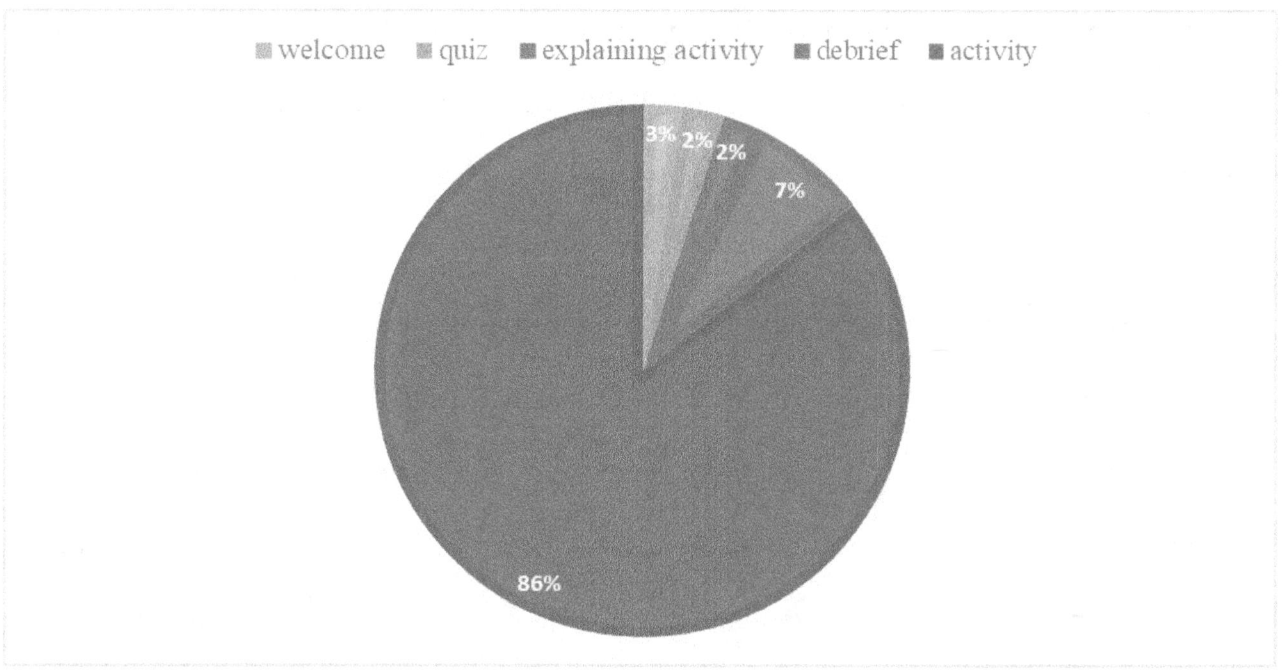

FIGURE 2: Suggested Structure of a 75-minute Class

PROS AND CONS AND ATTITUDE

The flipped classroom has caught the attention of both the teachers and the learners in the education field. This is because of the many advantages that it portrays. The most important and significant advantage is the augmented interactive period in the class. Since the lessons are introduced through lecture videos or audios or reading material, the teacher has time in the class which may be utilized for more student-teacher interaction and also the emotional demands of the students are taken care of which gives a better learning environment in the class. The students have a greater opportunity to discuss on a topic with their teacher as well as their peers thus giving scope to improve and hone their communication skills. This is not possible in a traditional classroom. Flipped classroom improves team work through collaborative approaches amongst the students and the teachers and teacher-students. Students can access the study material whenever and wherever giving independence and feasibility to work and learn at their own speed. The learning happens in a student-friendly environment without being threatened. The approach gives an impetus to the critical thinking skills and the creative thinking skills of the students. The refining of these 21st century skills helps the students in problem-solving and decision-making life skills.

Teachers can use a variety of teaching strategies increasing the teaching-learning spectrum. Parents are able to monitor and follow the courses taken by the students to give support when needed. A flipped class gives more time for innovations and research by the students. The students acquire meta-cognitive skills and collaborative learning strategies. There seems to be a statistical improvement in the vocabulary and grammar (Kang, 2015). It also has an immense positive effect on the confidence building, attitude, motivation, a sense of satisfaction, feeling towards the subject matter and the learning of the students. The collaborative approach improves the interpersonal skills thus giving the students the skills for people management.

The flip side of the coin is that the flipped classroom will fail to work with the effectiveness if the videos, audios and the reading material are of poor quality. The students may watch or go through the material amidst distractions at home which may hamper the effectiveness of the flipped approach. The increased learning responsibility of the students may leave them uncomfortable or give them a feeling abandon. Especially in a second language acquiring, students may want the instructor and the peers to answer questions on the videos, audios, etc. This may lead to the creation of disinterest towards the subject. Students accustomed to rote learning and lecture-style learning may be in for a culture shock and would put up a resistance to the increased responsibility of one's own learning. Not all teachers can prepare qualitative videos to create an impact the students. It increases the responsibility of the teachers. There may be unavoidable challenges like the students may not have the devices like smart phone, tabs or computers or may even have issues with internet and connectivity. The same applies for teachers too.

CONCLUSION

The effectiveness of a flipped classroom depends on whether the students go through the given material prior coming to class. The present-day millennials are digital-savvy which improves the congruence with the flipped class. Research has shown that there is more effect on the affective and inter-personal outcomes of the students. The active engagement and learner-centred activities and interactions need to be curated and designed by the instructors in a way that becomes an effective pedagogical practice. Being relatively a new concept, the research on the effectiveness of the flipped classroom is still growing. Research should also investigate and explore the relationship between the flipped classroom and the age, gender and students' level of knowledge. There should also be further research on the various forms of flipped classrooms and the relation with the learning outcomes, which will help in formulating pedagogical practices in the instructional development. There is a lot of scope for the flourishing of the flipped classroom.

REFERENCES

1. Al-Naabi, I.S., (2020). Is it Worth Flipping? The Impact of Flipped Classroom on EFL Students' Grammar, English Language Teaching; Vol. 13, No. 6; 2020 ISSN 1916-4742 E-ISSN 1916-4750 Published by Canadian Center of Science and Education.

2. Armbruster, P., Patel, M., Johnson, E. & Weiss, M. (2009) "Active Learning and Student-centered Pedagogy Improve Student Attitudes and Performance in Introductory Biology," CBE – Life Sciences Education, vol. 8, p. 203-213.

3. Baeten, M., et al (2010) "Using student-centred learning environments to stimulate deep approaches to learning: Factors encouraging or discouraging their effectiveness," Educational Research Review, vol. 5(3), p. 243-260.

4. Baker, J. W. (2000) "The 'classroom flip': Using web course management tools to become the guide by the side," 11th International Conference on College Teaching and Learning, Jacksonville, Florida, United States, April 12-15.

5. Bauer-ramazani, et al (2016). Flipped learning in TESOL: Definitions, approaches, and implementation. TESOL Journal, 7, 429–437. https://doi.org/10.1002/tesj.250.

6. Biggs, J. & Tang, C. (2007) Teaching for Quality Learning at University. Third Edition. The Society for Research into Higher Education. Open University Press.

7. Bishop, J. L., & Verleger, M. A., 2013. The Flipped Classroom: A Survey of the Research. 120th ASEE Annual Conference & Exposition. Atlanta: GA.

8. Butler, J.A. (1992) "Use of teaching methods within the lecture format," Medical Teacher, vol. 14(1), p. 11-25.

9. Butt, Adam. (2014). STUDENT VIEWS ON THE USE OF A FLIPPED CLASSROOM APPROACH: EVIDENCE FROM AUSTRALIA, BUSINESS EDUCATION & ACCREDITATION, Vol. 6 (1).

10. Frydenberg, Mark (2012). "Flipping Excel." Proceedings of the Information Systems Educators Conference, Volume 29, Number 1914, 1-11.

11. Flipped Learning Network (2014), What is a Flipped Learning? Retrieved from: http://fln.schoolwires.net/cms/lib07/VA01923112/Centricity/Domain/46/FLIP_handout_FNL_Web.pdf.

12. Garfield, J. (1995) "How Students Learn Statistics," International Statistical Review, Vol. 63(1), p. 25-34.

13. Jang, H.Y. and Kim H.J., (2020). A Meta-Analysis of the Cognitive, Affective, and Interpersonal Outcomes of Flipped Classrooms in Higher Education, Education Sciences.

14. Kong, S.C. Developing information literacy and critical thinking skills through domain knowledge learning in digital classrooms: An experience of practicing flipped classroom strategy. Comput. Educ. 2014, 78, 160–173.

15. Lage, M.J., Platt, G.J. & Treglia, M. (2000) "Inverting the classroom: A gateway to creating an inclusive learning environment," Journal of Economic Education, vol. 31(1), p. 30-43.

16. Milman, N., 2012. The flipped classroom strategy: what is it and how can it be used? Distance Learning, 9(3), 85- 87.

17. Mull B., 2012. Flipped learning: A response to five common criticisms. Retrieved from November Learning, 21 April, 2015.

18. Ozdamli, F., & Asiksoy, G, 2016. Flipped Classroom Approach, World Journal on Educational Technology: Current Issues Vol 8, Issue 2, (2016) 98-105.

19. Phillips, Cynthia R and Trainor, Joseph E., February, 2014. MILLENNIAL STUDENTS AND THE FLIPPED CLASSROOM, ASBBS Annual Conference: Las Vegas.

20. Sander, P., Stevenson, K., King, M. & Coates, D. (2000) "University Students' Expectations of Teaching," Studies in Higher Education, vol. 25(3), p. 309-323.

21. Smith, G. (1998) "Learning Statistics by Doing Statistics," Journal of Statistics Education, vol. 6(3), Article 04.

22. Toto, R., & Nguyen, H., 2009. Flipping the work design in an industrial engineering course. ASEE/IEEE Frontiers in Education Conference. San Antonio, TX.

VIRTUAL LEARNING AND CONFIDENCE BUILDING IN PUBLIC SPACE

Dr. Chinu Bohidar
Assistant Professor
Centurion University of Technology and Management
Odisha, India

INTRODUCTION

Education has changed drastically due to the COVID-19 Global Pandemic. The closure of schools and colleges worldwide has resulted in virtual learning. The use of different types of language apps, virtual tutorials, and online teaching platform has gone to a new level since the COVID- 19 pandemic. The new approach of learning has resulted in more productivity, flexibility, effective time management, active participation and maximum participants. A simple notification, meeting invitation and URL links can connect hundreds of participants to one canopy. The virtual platform has turned everyone to a speaker. The online platform has erased the hurdles between stage and the gallery. In speech communication, the speaker is exposed with the behaviour and body language of the audience or listeners, which is a form of obstacle in the process of communication. Lights, sounds, public gathering, technical noise, body language of the audience results in stage phobia, anxiety, nervousness, which aggregates poor speaking and lack of confidence among the people. This paper aims to find out the role of virtual learning in confidence building in public space. The paper will showcase how virtual learning helps students to speak and present their views on online platform; how sitting inside an airplane, sailing in a boat, driving the car one can deliver his/her speech without any physical proximity and anxiety.

Virtual learning has become an indispensable part of every student's life these days. Earlier, except for career interviews, online interaction was an unfamiliar concept for all. But the global pandemic shutdown has restored the entire learning process. Virtual classroom, virtual lab, online conference and webinar has hastened the learning process in this COVID-19 global pandemic. During the worldwide lockdown and shut down everything has come to a pause, but the online advance platforms and applications have accelerated the process of learning in this crisis. Imparting hassle-free education has become easy for online virtual software and application with amazing features. The unpredictable pandemic has forced everyone to stay at home and find alternatives for everything. The unanticipated pandemic has paved the way for many innovations and better alternatives. The digital learning which was never accepted earlier unconditionally and as a better way of communication, has now been accepted and adopted widely and graciously. Earlier also there were a number of communication tools with special features available, but except for a few companies' commercial organizations, they were not familiar and accepting the other way of communication except face-to-face communication.

THE NEW FACE OF LEARNING

The Prime Minister Narendra Modi declared the first lockdown in India on 22 March, 2020. It was followed by mandatory lockdowns in COVID-19 hotspots and all major cities. Further, on 24 March the prime minister ordered a nationwide lockdown for 21 days. The unforeseen lock down affected the entire 1.3 billion-people of India. When the process started lingering, experts and academician started exploring online learning platforms and its alternatives. Some ignored it, some accepted excitedly, some started criticizing, some started exploring, but people finally realised, this is the only alternative of learning in this catastrophe. In the opening, both the teacher and the learner found it difficult to adapt to online learning. The mindset of learning was difficult to shift from traditional classroom to computer-based learning. But with the flow of time both teacher and students have learnt the innovative way of online learning and its features.

Video lectures, flip classroom, group chat, video conference, augmented reality and virtual reality have taken the standard of learning to a new height. Individual learning has resulted in content adjustment, personalised learning, identification of own strengths and weaknesses among the learners. Recorded classes, video lectures, animated videos, and virtual images have resulted in flexible learning with maximum retention. It has further helped students in effective time management. Personal computer and android phone have turned into physical classroom; whiteboard, computer lab and digital screen may be accessed in just simple clicks. The halt in time consumption in movement, campus activity and academic exercises have paved the ways for more academic concentration and in-depth learning.

THE COMFORT ZONE

For many students, school is a place of fear, anxiety and competition. The online mode of learning allows students to work individually. It helps students to explore and showcase their capabilities. With the flow of time, students have learnt the online antiques, which has helped individual students to speak and present their topics freely and confidently. Lack of physical proximity has intensified hassle-free and flawless speaking power. In school fixed hour, students get distracted by many other activities but in an online platform it is more flexible and more productive. In group learning all students have to run with the same speed. They do not get the scope to repeat a lesson and clear their doubts. But virtual learning help students to see their recorded classes and clear their doubts any moment. At online school, students learn in their comfortable surroundings. Students can customise their learning-plan and assignments as per their convenience. The presence of audience sometimes creates anxiety and fear amongst the speakers while delivering a speech. A simple task may turn to a complex and hard speech if the audience involves experts, judges and senior member of the related field. But in online learning when the audience are just a name or email id it becomes easy on the part of the speaker to deliver his/her speech with confidence.

AUDIENCE AND PERFORMANCE

There are few people who are born confident public speakers. But nervousness, fear, anxiety and tension are some of the common behavioural characteristics among people when they speak in public space. These are the common symptoms everyone faces at some point of their life. There are some who always love to speak in public. But whenever the size of the audience is large and speaker has to prove or motivate the audience and the speaker will be judged by a team of experts, nervousness and fear become a common phenomenon. Earlier studies reveal that there is relation between audience and performance (cf.Geen & Gange, 1977). Audience presence enhances drive arousal which in turn enhances dominant responses. Zajonc (1980) and other studies have shown that audience impact depends on factors as degree of evaluation, audience expertness, audience familiarity and sex of the audience. The fear of public results in poor communication skill and lack of confidence building on the part of the speaker. In early schooling, public speaking and communication skill does not play much role. But during higher education and university level education, better communication skill and public speaking become an important part of academic. To excel in their professional career, students during their higher studies should mainly focus on speaking in meeting, conference and seminar. Good scope in exploring and building communication skill helps students to grow in their later stage of life. Though there are many tips and strategies suggested by the experts to deal with anxiety in public speaking, it is very difficult on the part of the speaker to overcome from anxiety and fear before and during the speech in public.

To overcome the fear and anxiety among people, public speaking should be a part of school curriculum right from school and university level.

VIRTUAL LEARNING AND PUBLIC SPEAKING

Man is a social animal whose behaviour changes profoundly as per different situation and people. Surrounding and people stimulates the behaviour and way of speaking of an individual. People behave differently in private and public places. The speaker decides where he/she needs to be introvert and blunt. Earlier studies reveal that the intensity of the audience and the size of the room has a relation with the speakers. People speak confidently when they are in their comfort zones. When we are alone and within our own private space, it gives more confidence to the speakers to deliver a speech on a given topic. The same happens with virtual learning, people are in their comfort zones, though the number of participants is large, due to lack of physical proximity, speaker feels comfortable and free of stress and anxiety. Virtual platform equips speakers with no interference and immediate feedback during the process of speech. The mute option, raise hand, screen sharing, message box and no video options bring more comfort for the speaker. Before COVID-19 pandemic, it was bit difficult for the people to realise that meetings, interactions, agreements, conferences can be done so smoothly on a virtual platform. People took little time to accept the reality in the initial stage. The unpredictable global pandemic forced everyone to work from home and be an expert in online platform. Now every personal laptop, desktop and android mobile is equipped with online applications like, Zoom, Skype, Google Meet, Impartus, Jio Chat, Teams, Lifesize, Twitch and many more. Now all professionals and students have learned the virtual meeting etiquettes. Now the host of a meeting where more than 500 people are audience can keep the entire meeting room quiet in just one click. The receiver's feedback can be controlled by the host with just one click. In physical public speaking, feedback is a continuous process and sometimes create hurdles in the process of communication, which can now be controlled digitally by the organizer or the host of the meeting.

NOISE: THE BARRIER OF COMMUNICATION

Noise is an unwanted signal which obstructs the process of communication. It is a type of barrier in the process of communication. Noise is present in all types of communication. Noise usually comes from the channel.

There are mainly two types of noise, which is usually produced in the external and internal sources. In all forms of communication both types of noise can create disturbance in the flow of communication. In virtual communication, both types of noise sometimes create disturbance. People, usually in public speaking platform get diverted by eye contact, lack of attention, vacant seat, conversation amongst the members of the audiences. All this symbolic feedback of the receiver form noise and obstacle in the process of speech delivery. In virtual communication these types of external noise usually do not occur. But technical noise like network issue, power breakup, unwanted noise from participants are some of the problems which arise in virtual communication process.

Internal Noise can be psychological and semantic in nature. Internal noise is the result of anxiety, nervousness, stress and tension. In virtual conversation, internal noise can be eliminated to a large extent, due to lack of physical closeness. When a speaker concentrates on his presentation and starts speaking, he is alone inside a vacant room. The audience or the receiver are just a name there, for the speaker.

VIRTUAL MEETING ETIQUETTE

Due to Covid-19 pandemic when everything changed suddenly, people took time to absorb the reality. Slowly people started accepting the importance of social distancing. Virtual meeting, video conference, online classes are no longer a new concept for people. In a very short span of time people of all age groups have learnt the techniques, features and utilization of virtual world.

In the beginning, of the global pandemic when all professionals and students started downloading and installing the online meeting software, except for few, most of the professionals were unaware about virtual meeting. Gradually people started exploring the features with in it. In the beginning people become silent spectators and then they become active participants. Everyday use of virtual platform has made the people learn etiquettes of virtual meeting.

Having continuously attending virtual meetings, people have learnt scheduling a meeting, punctuality, muting the microphone, silent space, overlapping of voice etc. The virtual etiquette plays an important role for a fruitful meeting. A professionally arranged meeting boosts the host and other participants to act professionally and smoothly. A hassle-free virtual meeting with good network connection, audio-visual quality and efficient organiser improves the confidence of the speaker.

CONCLUSION

The Covid-19 global pandemic has changed the face of the entire world. Before the pandemic when everything was normal people had never thought of virtual world so seriously. All these features people currently using was available earlier too. But society had always preferred face to face conversation and meeting people physically. Except for international meetings and professional interviews people never utilised the already existing software from their smart phones and computers. But the social distancing concept has forced all, to realise the power of virtual world. The unpredictable virus has compelled everyone to use the virtual platform despite being in a same building. The ongoing virtual form of communication has made everyone a good speaker. A study table has now turned to a stage and a URL link has converted a smart phone screen to a class. The crowded hall with howling sounds which fasten the heartbeat and the stress of a speaker has disappeared now. Loud speaker, microphone, halogen light is no more there to initiate the stage phobia. One is free to speak as if someone is speaking to the mirror. The speaker need not worry much about how he/she appears and how his/her body language should be. Everyone concentrates only on what he/she speaks as a speaker.

REFERENCES:

1. Guerin, B. (1986). Mere Presence Effects in Humans: A review. *Journal Of Experimental Social Psychology*, *22*(1), 38-77. doi: 10.1016/0022-1031(86)90040-5

2. Morris, W., Walden, H., Walden, H., & Fogel, A. (2020). Virtual Meeting Etiquette: Everything You Need to Know to Go Remote. Retrieved 11 October 2020, from https://www.elegantthemes.com/blog/business/virtual-meeting-etiquette-everything-you-need-to-know-to-go-remote

3. Noise. (2020). Retrieved 11 October 2020, from https://www.daenotes.com/electronics/communication-system/noise

4. Noise and Interference: Public Speaking/Speech Communication. (2020). Retrieved 11 October 2020, from https://lumen.instructure.com/courses/218897/pages/linkedtext54121?module_item_i

d=5006937#:~:text=Noise%20and%20interference%20block%20the,to%20send%20a
s%20you%20speak.

5. What are the four different types of noise? | Cirrus Research. (2020). Retrieved 11 October 2020, from https://www.cirrusresearch.co.uk/blog/2020/04/4-different-types-noise/

LEARNING IN THE VIRTUAL SPACE: CHALLENGES AND OPPORTUNITIES

Dr. Ambika Sankar Mishra
Associate Professor
Centurion University of Technology and Management
Odisha, India

INTRODUCTION

Education is considered as the backbone of a democratic society. For the better future of a democratic society, education is highly essential. The process of educating never ends with teaching rather it is completed with learning. The process of learning is completed by internalization of the subjects and their application in everyday life. The new generation students are quite different by their attitude and they are highly techno savvy. Learning through the classroom teaching has become a task of boredom for them and at the same time, they want education to be imparted in an attractive and interactive form.

Wilber Schramm in his famous book *"Mass Media and national development"* (1964) says "Light is better than darkness and knowledge is better than ignorance". So, knowledge is an essential requirement for human beings to survive in a society and education is the means for knowledge. Socrates speaks "Education is the kindling of a flame, not the filling of a vessel". It means education should be provided in such a way that it should inspire the students to gain more and more knowledge. It should help them to empower themselves by learning skills of life. It should help them to solve the challenges of life with the knowledge they have received from their education.

While discussing the above, we understand it that education is an essential requirement for the survival, growth and development of an individual in any society. If education is imparted in a proper way to fulfill the requirements of life, then the individual and the society survive in a better way. A properly imparted education perfectly shapes the personality of an individual making him aware about his and other's human rights. Real education never solves the problems for the person in a real-life situation but it empowers him to solve his own life problems in a skillful manner. So, in other words, proper education promotes empowerment in a learner and enlightens him. In the contemporary social and educational scenario of India, imparting quality and meaningful education has various challenges and there is a need of removing these obstacles from the path. The basic problems which work like road blocks in imparting meaningful education are:

Language: Language as a medium of communication plays a crucial role in exchange of ideas and information. In Indian context, India is a multilingual country and at the same time there is not enough scope for the students in India to learn other languages than the mother tongue. However, the arrival of modern mass media has made Hindi popular in almost all the corners of the country but still the Indian students suffer from linguistic barriers till date. The popularisation of English education and development of English as a window language at the world level has raised new challenges in front of the Indian educationists and students. Though speaking and writing of English are no more challenges to urban students but the same issue has remained as a challenge to the students of rural India, which lacks from public schools and well-trained teachers to impart English education in a better way. Both urban and rural students are equally talented but due to the constraint of English language, students from rural background suffer more than urban students.

Lack of Communication Skills: Communication skills are one among the important requirements for imparting meaningful education among our students. Having only knowledge is meaningless for a person if he/she is not able to express it properly at the time of need.

Banking Concept of Education: Present educational system prevalent in our country is only based on the concept of retention of information and it is not much efficient to promote learning or developing life skills in a student. To speak in a better way if we analyse our present educational scenario, we will find it that our educational system has a large amount of similarities with that of "Banking concept of education" conceptualised in Freirean pedagogy. In the banking concept of education, the teacher holds a key position and the student never becomes a part of the educational system, which hinders learning. The process of learning is not participatory. It is completely authoritarian where the teacher imposes everything, and the students work with the illusion of learning though they never become a part of the learning process. Thus, the banking concept of education has the least scope for learning and at the same time, the banking concept of education being authoritarian and suppressive, kills the interest of students towards learning.

The Teaching vs Preaching Debate: Teaching as a noble profession is involved with imparting knowledge within the students but in India most of the teachings are purely classroom based having no practical demonstration of the subjects. Again learning through observation and experimentation is too low in case of Indian teaching system. The classroom teaching in which the teacher goes on talking about subjects without creating realisation among students also creates a problem for students to understand it and decreases the value of the education. Lack of practical demonstration and active participation between teacher and students is making the process of learning less interesting by changing the status of a teacher to a preacher.

Communicative Ecology and Traditional Knowledge System: Earlier while talking about communication, we have defined it as a process of human experience which plays a crucial role in information dissemination in the process of teaching. Culture as a part of the communicative ecology plays a crucial role to make communication process meaningful for imparting education. As India is a multicultural country so the communicative ecology is different from one place to another and it works as a big obstacle in imparting meaningful education. For example, each society has its own model for educating its individuals and this traditional way of imparting knowledge has worked successfully for years among different communities. But before introducing any new approach to the learning system to make the process of learning more meaningful there should be a proper understanding of the traditional knowledge system and cultural values of society.

Thus, when Indian educational scenario is surrounded by such road blocks there is a need and necessity of strategic intervention to solve the problems of the educational system. Education should be designed in such a manner that it should bring critical consciousness among the students so that they can solve their problems by the knowledge they have acquired. In a better way following the Chinese proverb, it can be said "Give a man a fish and he eats for a day; help him learn how to fish, and he eats for life". Education should solve this purpose by igniting inner talents of the students. To satisfy the purpose of a meaningful education, it should be imparted in an attractive and fascinating manner. In an era when we are chatting about edutainment with slogans like "Karlo Duniya Muthi Main" and when android phones have started reaching to the vibrant new generation and the youth of this country have started loving technology the technology in itself is a solution to such problem.

With the repaid growth of technology, we have reached to an era in which a sim card is cheaper than 1kilo rice, Mobile phones are sold with offers during festivals like dresses, our food is from Swiggy or Zomato, our travel depends on OLA or Uber, our clothes are from Myntra, our medicines are from netmed.com, our grocery shop is amazon, our fruit and vegetables are from bigbasket.com. our restaurant waiter or exam invigilator is a robot and along with Artificial intelligence and machine learning, we have started living in an era of man machine interface. Our relationships have gone shifted to virtual platforms and relationships in the physical environment are pushed to the corner. Our money has become the plastic money, our book has turned to the e-reader and our pen these days is the voice to text keyboard or the paint brush is the joystick. Thus, the society surrounding us has changed, the cultural patterns have changed and our involvements with the social institutions have changed.

Thus, in such an environment of artificial intelligence and augmented reality or virtual reality we have started living in the environment of new educational and information technology and as a user centric and democratic platform, it has brought changes in the communicative behavior of its users.

LEARNING IN THE VIRTUAL SPACE

We have started living in a society in which augmented reality, virtual reality, artificial intelligence, automation, internet of things and machine learning have started becoming the new areas to fascinate human life and inquisitiveness of researchers. The man machine interface has become a new area to explore and we have started reaching to the era of rise of the machines. In this Digital era, a sim card is cheaper than a Kilo of rice and Swiggy or Zomato are the managers of our food. Byju's or Udemy are the managers of our education. WhatsApp or Facebook are our new communication platforms for information dissemination. Coding has started becoming the new language of modern society and social network analysis has become the tool to analyse the communication behavior of human beings. For all our needs we have started depending on the digital systems but this digital life or the life in the virtual space has placed challenges for us. The fast-moving life in the present days and the rapid growth in information technology has shifted our lives from physical space to virtual space. With each new sunrise, human race is moving one more step towards the virtual life and the growth of technology has moved to such a level that the tiny portable mobile devices have started controlling our lives. The small screen has started replacing the big screen and wireless system has started replacing the wires. In the Indian context, with the hopes of 5G round the corner the wireless hopes have gone stronger. The new generation mobile savvy students are more interested to carry education in their pocket than running to the classroom. During the pandemic when we are flattening the curve and attempting to increase the distance in the physical life, our education system has shifted to a virtual platform. Education in a virtual platform has proved that

- it is participatory and the rate of involvement of audience is very high.

- audience has maximum opportunity to play the role of communicator and receiver.

- it has ample opportunities for interaction.

- it is a new and an attractive form of communication.

- it creates a virtual world to provide a better satisfaction in communication.

- communicator and respondent are known to each other.

- individual members of the audience are mostly linked with a similar cultural background which makes the communication more effective.

Education in virtual space with above advantages and with its audio-visual contents has become the potential new medium of today and it has started satisfying the uses and gratification perspective of people in a powerful manner. Education in the virtual space is highly user friendly due to its interesting features. It actually promotes the educational environment in a better manner due to the following advantages.

Economic Aspect: Education in the virtual space is not expensive because initially it may look expensive but in long run it is cheaper than the education in physical environment. Similarly, students get opportunity to learn from best teachers which helps in enhancing their knowledge.

Anytime, Anywhere Available: Education in virtual space is highly user friendly and the information is available at any place at any time.

New Way of Imparting Education: This new form of education has opened up new ways for teaching and learning. With the advent of augmented reality and virtual reality, the students are no meek listeners rather they are able to get the real time experience to work with the teacher while learning different subjects. learning is no more restricted to printed books or materials rather list of learning materials have gone extended to video lectures and demonstrations starting from online study material. The open educational resources have started providing learning materials at free of cost. Learning with the infotainment technique has become interesting and the education has gone more and more attractive.

LMS and EXS: Learning in the virtual platform is no more restricted to content production. To make it organised, thinkers working for the enhancement of virtual life, have started planning properly to regulate the content production and distribution system in the modern virtual educational system. The introduction of learning management system (LMS) is a result of such effort. Today we have beautifully customized LMS platforms to provide education in a well-designed and well-structured manner. Similarly, due to the introduction of EXS, learning has gone more and more effective.

Respectful Way of Learning: People learn best when they are treated properly and are not humiliated or treated as ignorant. Learning on the virtual platform helps the students to explore to the maximum and they are no more restricted to the knowledge available in the book or the knowledge available with the teacher which creates self-awareness for the learner. There are the least possible scopes to get humiliated. Similarly, the idea of school phobia is not there on the virtual learning platform rather the school comes to the learner at her/his wish.

No Restriction of Time and Promotes Self-learning: Virtual learning encourages self-learning without the constraint of time thus it becomes more and more useful for the learner to explore more and more into the depth of knowledge.

Peer-learning: It never restricts peer learning rather through different virtual groups and virtual associations it promotes peer learning and at the same time it promotes in knowledge sharing and knowledge distribution in a larger environment to add more and more credibility for the learner.

Instant Rewards or Help: Virtual learning is highly capable to provide instant leaning or help and at the same time as the online medium is a medium to respond very fast that is why the feedback to any of the contents posted is received very soon. This helps the learner to rectify mistakes quickly and get feedback on his work at the least time.

 Self-evaluation: Virtual platform helps in self-evaluation and at the same time it helps in self-exploration thus it is a powerful way of imparting education.

CHALLENGES

Education in the virtual space has not advantages only because each lamp also has a dark side also. The biggest challenge to education in the virtual space is the internet connection and available bandwidth because without the proper availability of internet bandwidth and due to lack of proper internet connection online education suffers a lot. Similarly choosing the proper content for the purpose of enhancing knowledge is also another challenge. The internet is just like the ocean of knowledge and choosing the proper content from internet is also another challenge to move ahead to get knowledge. Similarly getting friendly with technology is also another need and it also acts like a challenge in the online education.

CONCLUSION

In Indian scenario after the pandemic the number of instances of using online platform for education have increased a lot and it has started changing the scenario. Looking towards the situation, telecom companies have started playing a major role. Thus, these days the learners have started using it in a more and more manner and if we will look into the modern learners, then we can realize that with smartphones in their hands they have started gathering knowledge for their own need. Education has started becoming more and more interest oriented than a compulsion. Thus, there is a necessity to understand the preferences and habits of the new age learners. The virtual learning system has brought a magical change in our educational system and has brought a rapid change with lots of challenges for us.

REFERENCES:

1. Schramm,Wilber (1964) Mass Media and National Development, Stanford University Press, Freire, Paulo (2005) Pedagogy of the oppressed, The Continuum International Publishing Group New York, NY 10010

2. Singhal,Aravind; Roger,Everett M (2000) India's Communication revolution, Sage Publications Newdelhi

3. http://www.unesco.org/education/aladin/paldin/pdf/course01/unit_13.pdf.

4. http://eprints.lse.ac.uk/42947/1/__libfile_repository_Content_Livingstone,%20S_Critical%20reflections_Livingstone_Critical%20reflections_2014.pdf.

5. https://commons.princeton.edu/inclusivepedagogy/wp-content/uploads/sites/17/2016/07/freire_pedagogy_of_the_oppresed_ch2-3.pdf.

6. https://www.igi-global.com/dictionary/embedding-ecology-notion-social-production/4676.

7. https://www.thesocialmediahat.com/blog/7-characteristics-of-a-successful-social-media-presence/

INTEGRATING MULTIPLE STRATEGIES FOR IMPROVING READING COMPREHENSION

Dr. Amir Prasad Behera
Assistant Professor
Centurion University of Technology and Management
Odisha, India

INTRODUCTION

This chapter provides an overview of the research into the development of a learner's reading comprehension skills through a learning platform, provides innovative learning solutions that drive better outcomes for educational organisations. It is a platform to enrich existing programs by extending the classroom for online students. It is a great way to hold read aloud and virtual comprehension discussions with students. The chapter is about virtual comprehension activities that can be implemented now and in the future. It is an interactive process as a transaction between the reader and the author through the text. The reader's capabilities, abilities, knowledge, and experiences affect the act of reading (Supono, 2009). The chapter aims to integrate platform for improving reading comprehension of learners. The study is completely descriptive. Data gained from this study can be used by language teachers and educators to support the reading comprehension of English language learners in their schools, colleges and universities. This will improve the vocabulary which will lead towards the improvement of the language ability and communication skills. The findings of the study show that integrating of platform in teaching and learning enhances the reading comprehension of the students. The findings are based on the data collected from class at Centurion University of Technology and Management.

There are several skills involved when one learns a second or foreign language. Syille-Troike (2006) defines two types of skills, such as receptive (reading and listening) and productive (writing and speaking). The first is stated by the written mode and the latter by verbal communication. From these, it is understood that reading is a crucial skill for students of English as a second language (ESL) and English as a foreign language (EFL) because it may lead to greater development in other academic areas, and students believe that reading is very essential skill to master their career (Anderson, 1999).

In order to guide students to become better readers, Mikulecky (2011) explains that teachers of English as a second and foreign language need to give more emphasis in teaching skills because this will help students to better comprehend English language texts. Grabe (2009), among other researchers, has examined the effectiveness of instruction of a number of different strategies to improve reading comprehension, for example, identifying important information, making guesses about unknown words, building main-idea summaries, skimming and scanning.

Thus, this study was carried out with the purpose of ascertaining whether platform could be introduced in order to help students achieve the goal of improving reading comprehension. Becoming better and more efficient readers is very crucial for students when they are studying in a discipline and preparing to begin their careers. They should have the ability to read another language which could help them to get a job of a higher standard. The present study was intended to analyse the effectiveness of the use of the platform in order to gather more evidence to support the claim that they enhance students' English reading ability. Moreover, this study aims to address a further notion: whether or not the use of this interactive technological platform could have the potential for making the input more comprehensible and, thus, facilitating students to improve their reading ability.

As such, the present study was guided by the following research question: Does integrating platform make the Reading Comprehension more effective? This research study was conducted taking 1st Year and 2nd year batch students of 2020 academic year of Centurion University of Technology and Management, Odisha, India. The study was monitored in a Job Readiness Course. A case study methodology was used to explore the different perceptions students had about platform online Job Readiness Class. Six main perceptions concerning the platform: its content delivery and objectives; its level of difficulty, the time invested in the platform, adults' learning, and the role of the teacher - were mainly investigated.

THE OBJECTIVE OF THE STUDY

The objective of this study was to explore the different perceptions students have about an English reading comprehension class on the Platform.

READING COMPREHENSION

Reading is linguistic processes which are defined as a complex mixture of rapid, efficient, comprehending, interactive, strategic, flexible, purposeful, evaluative, and learning. (Grabe, 2009). Furthermore, reading comprehension is defined as finding and creating meaning in a simultaneous way and it has three components: (a) The person who comprehends the text called the reader (b) The written symbols to be comprehended are called as the text, and last component is the activity that the person carries out in order to comprehend the text. These three components are interconnected and such interaction is the determining factor to create successful reading comprehension (Polselli & Snow, 2003). The process of reading is a communication as it connects the author and the reader. Through reading, the reader gains knowledge and information thus it is an active or receptive rather than a passive skill.

IMPARTUS PLATFORM

This a simple and comprehensive, learning platform that brings about a paradigm shift in the teaching - learning experience. With the help of platform, educators are able to capture, edit, and distribute contextually relevant content. Students get deeper opportunities to watch recorded or live-streamed class lectures and review all the course material at any time, from anywhere. The platform serves more students with existing resources while improving outcomes for all. This is a platform where teacher can supervise student's attendance, assign different task and quizzes, share screen, record his teaching and in the back pack of the platform teacher upload question bank, teacher's handouts, PPTs and PDFs. All these facilities of the platform make the teaching and learning process more comfortable and flexible.

The core features include the followings:

• Multi-view Automated Lecture Capture

• In-Video Search

• Discussion Forum

• Flipped Lectures

• Video Conferencing and Live Streaming

• Sharing of Screen

LITERATURE REVIEW

Grabe (2009) states, the key to good reading either in the first or second language are the effective use of reading strategies. However, the process differs slightly with second language reading strategies since they involve issues that are not included in the first language, such as, mental translations, first language transfer, and the metacognitive advantage of second language readers. However, as the present study was intended to determine whether

Centurion University students perceive the use of platform strategies as effective to improve. Facilitators always should   monitor technological comprehension with different strategies in order to know student's comprehension. In the platform reader uses both technological and mental ability to do the reading comprehension exercises.

Mangen et al. (2013) also investigated effects of the technological interface on reading comprehension in Norwegian school. Their study found that the students who read texts in print scored significantly better on the reading comprehension test than students who read the texts on the computer screen. It has been also found from different research study that participants doing reading comprehension experience higher levels of experienced stress and tiredness than those who read from paper.

It is concluded that in paper-based and computer-based reading methods, more exploration is required to know the effectiveness of reading performance. In this 21st century, tablets have become other user-friendly reading devices for teaching and learning process because it is a book-like device with great portability, usability, and interactivity. Zhang et al. (2014) have proposed a new familiarity questionnaire in order to measure tablet familiarity. In their studies they have found that students are more familiars with the use of tablets. Hence, it is required to evaluate reading performance among different media platforms in order to know and understand the effectiveness of different platforms.

The reading comprehension can be classified into two levels, literal level and inferential level (McNamara 2007; Wagner et al. 2009). Literal comprehension, also called the shallow comprehension, is a minimally coherent mental representation which is achieved by readers from the meaning of the explicit knowledge in the text (McNamara 2007). On the other hand, inferential comprehension, namely the deep comprehension, represents a highly coherent, richly integrated, plausible presentation. The readers can use the explicit knowledge in the text and their own prior knowledge to build deeper understanding from the text (McNamara 2007).

Different methods were used to measure the levels of reading comprehension. Some researchers designed the closed-end questions, such as multiple-choice questions, to exam students' literal comprehension. In contrast, in order to examine the inferential comprehension, the open-end questions, such as summarization or short-answer questions, were designed to reorganize the deep process of the text.

CONTEXT

In order to improve English Language and Communication Skill Centurion University of Technology and Management, Odisha has introduced Job Readiness Course for graduate students on platform modality. In this Reading Comprehension module covers the major portion of the course. The complete duration of the course is 28 hours. It has 3 modules. Each module is of 7 hours.   The Reading Comprehension module of the course Job Readiness explores topics such as words and their meaning, reading strategies, development of reading skills, methods of text organization and critical reading and includes different tools such as forums and chats to discuss course content, videos to provide explanations about the topics and content of the course, questionnaires and links to other websites to provide exercises and practice using platform. In the present study the effectiveness of the platform is explored and suggestion and recommendations are given for further improvements of the platform.

PARTICIPANTS

The students who participated in this study were from Schools of Centurion University of Technology and Management. This research study was done taking students of Centurion University of Technology and Management because they were the students who were having the reading comprehension module in the Job Readiness Course offered by the university to certify language competence and communication skill. The course is offered for 2000 students. But the study has been done taking 100 students from different batches. Their ages ranged from 19 to 22. They were enrolled in different graduate programs such as Bachelor of Science, Bachelor of Technology, Master of Science, and Pharmaceutical and Engineering etc. Regarding their experience taking platform courses, only few students said they had taken courses in this modality of instruction related and others for the first time use this platform for their class.

DATA COLLECTION

The data related to the effectiveness of platform in Reading Comprehension class was gathered from survey questionnaire. Although the instruments were designed to learn of the students' use of reading strategies, motivation, and perceptions such as difficulties with the platform, time invested material and the role of the teacher, it was decided to use only the information regarding to the perceptions the students had about the platform for the purpose of this study. The questionnaires were used in order to make sure that students understood and answered the questions clearly and felt comfortable sharing their perceptions and feelings towards the platform on reading comprehension.

The questionnaire included open and close ended questions. The questionnaire was published on the platform of the course, where the students could download it, fill it in, and upload it again to the platform. In other case the students sent the questionnaire to the teacher's e-mail address. When the course was ended, a survey was carried out to know the students' perceptions of the process: the platform, the teacher, the contents, their motivation and their reading comprehension process.

TABLE: 1.1 Survey Questionnaire on the Use of Impartus

Sl. No.	Questions	Give tick mark as per your choice	
1	Is the online platform user friendly?	Yes	No
2.	Does the use of platform improve reading, writing, listening and speaking skill?	Yes	No
3.	Does the use of platform improve the Reading Comprehension ability?	Yes	No
4.	Does the Reading Comprehension exercise improve language abilities?	Yes	No
5.	Does the role of facilitator helpful for improving Reading Comprehension Skill?	Yes	No
6.	How useful are the chats, forums, and instant messages in the class?	Yes	No
7.	Does the Polling option in the Impartus create interest among the students?	Yes	No
8.	Does the platform improve the creativity of the students?	Yes	No
9.	Is the Impartus platform class better than the paper-based class?	Yes	No
10.	Is Impartus platform class interactive?	Yes	No

FINDINGS AND DISCUSSIONS

As already mentioned, this study focuses on identifying the perceptions or opinions of the students after participating in an online platform class. The study found six main topics of student perceptions concerning the course: its content and objectives; its level of difficulty, the time invested, the role of the teacher and adult learning. The summary of the finding is given in Table 1.2.

TABLE 1.2: The Summary of the Findings

Aspect	Perception
Activities and Advantages of the Course	User friendly platform Use of chats, forums, and instant messages to ensure an interactive communication with the teacher and students
Level of Difficulty	Higher than expected at the beginning of the course Very demanding
Time Invested	The platform is highly time consuming
Teacher's Usefulness and Facilitation	Constant teacher support The teacher becomes a technical expert and an immediate feedback provider (Muñoz & González, 2010).
Course Content and Objectives	The course was expected to be grammar-based The readings of the course were expected to be about law The course was expected to deal with the skimming, scanning, note-making, filling up the gaps, jumbled sentence and jumbled paragraph
Adult Learning Process	The participants in the course thought their ages would hinder their learning process

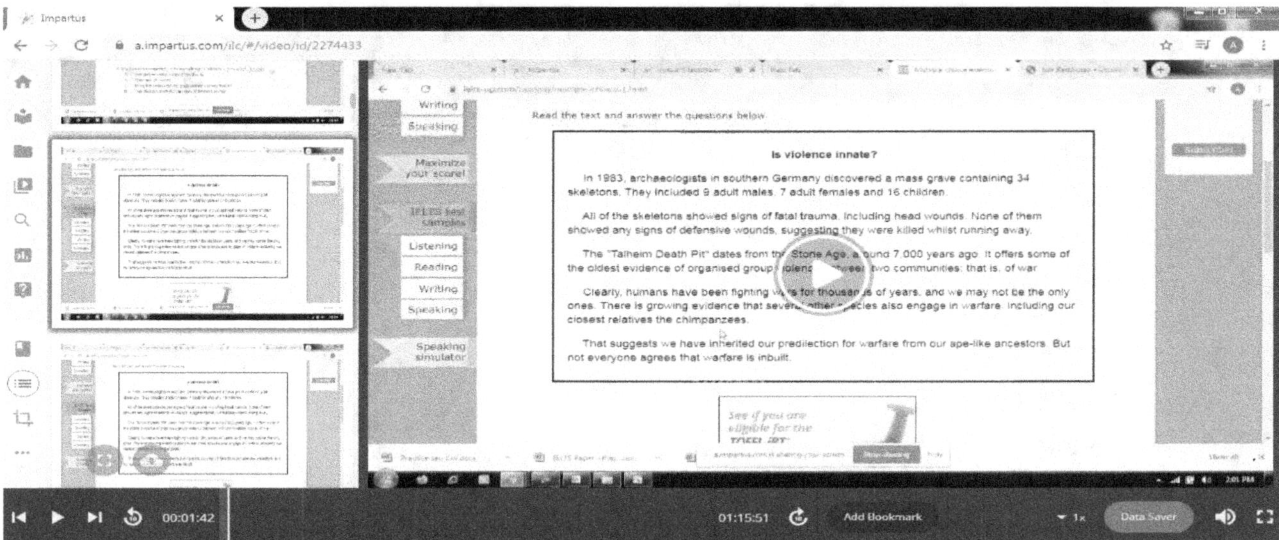

FIGURE 1.1: Reading Comprehension Exercise (Screenshot of the Class)

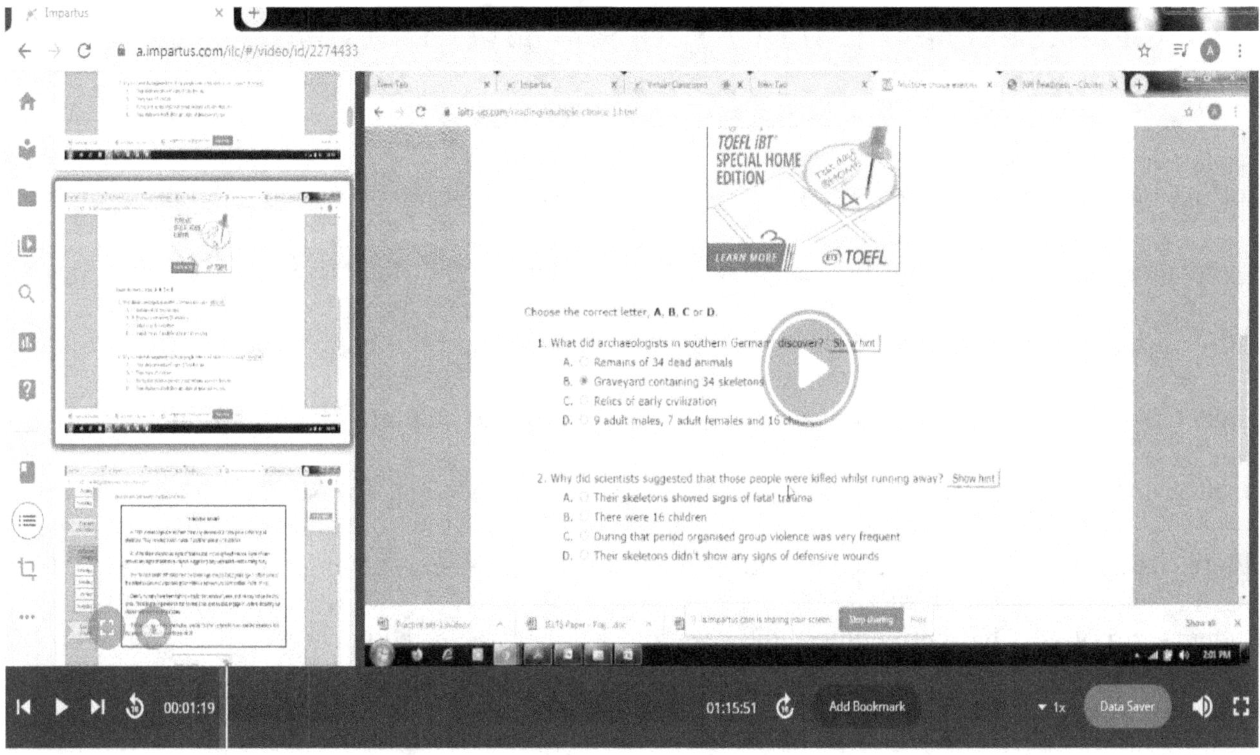

FIGURE 1.2: Question and Answer (Screenshot of the Class)

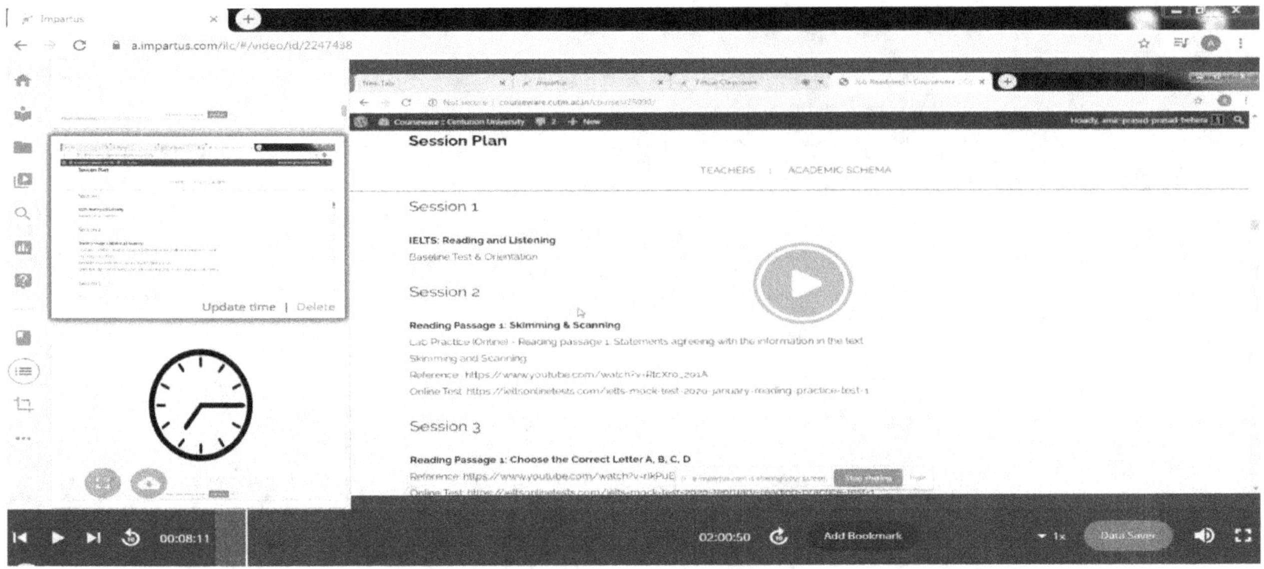

FIGURE 1.3: Question on Skimming and Scanning (Screenshot of the Class)

PARTICIPANTS FEEDBACK ABOUT TOOLS, ACTIVITIES AND ADVANTAGES OF THE COURSE

The participants of the study reported several perceptions about the tools, activities and advantages that the platform offered. After taking the course, the students mentioned that the platform has several positive features: it was user friendly and the communication with the teacher was fluid. They pointed out the use of the forum, the chat and the e-mail in order to discuss, topics related to the course content, to share knowledge, to ask questions and to obtain feedback from the teacher and sometimes from other students. However, some students reported that sometimes the e-mail was more effective than the chat for communication. They also highlighted the implementation of tutorial videos to explain the content of the course.

Topics related to the course content, to share knowledge, to ask questions and to obtain feedback from the teacher and sometimes from other students. However, some students reported that sometimes the e-mail was more effective than the chat for communication. They also highlighted the implementation of tutorial videos to explain the content of the course.

For example, Nabneet, a student of B.Sc. (Ag.), 2nd year given response in the survey questionnaire that "With the use of the platform, we get to know about our mistakes which we are committing during our test in Google form and with the help of our teachers it is being rectified."

Following are the other responses from other different students:

Participant 6: During our classes on we sometimes get to practice different questions of reading, writing and also in Google platform our performing efficiency is increasing.

Participant 7: Different online mock tests like IELTS and other tests improve the reading comprehension, and teacher's guidance helps improve reading ability.

Participant 9: There are many things which are helpful for the students for example chat box where we can write and clear our doubts, there are also mic options and video options where we can share anything and also the polling system is more interesting.

The students pinpointed that the course has several advantages: They indicated that this modality of instruction allows the students to manage their own time; they do not have to go to a specific place to attend a class or any other event, the teaching. Process is personalised because it is always available on the internet and there is constant and direct contact with the teacher or instructor.

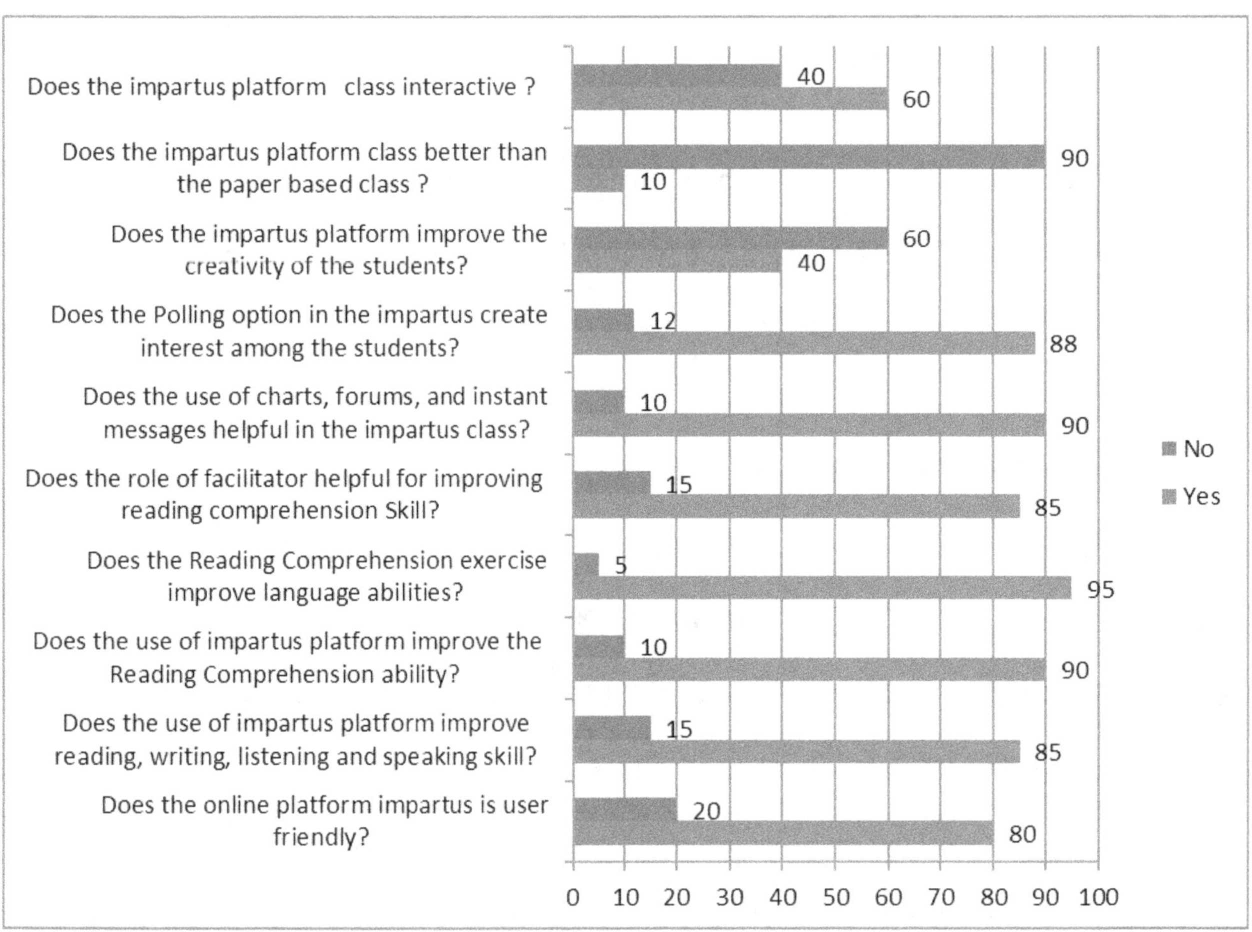

FIGURE 1.4: Findings of the Survey Questionnaire

In order to know the effectiveness of the reading comprehension class a survey was done taking 100 students of Centurion University of Technology and Management, Odisha, India. The result of the survey is displayed in the above graph (Figure 1.4). The graph displays that out of 100 students 60 students say that the platform is interactive and 40 students say it is not interactive. This is a platform where both the teacher and students can effectively interact with each other. 90% students say this platform is better than paper-based platform. As this platform is virtual, it lacks real class room environment. Often it needs network to have classes. But it in real class all can see each other and know each other state of being. So, the platform reading comprehension is not so effective than paper base class.

The graph also presents the response about the creativity of the students. According the result of the graph it is understood that 60 say that in the platform they lack creativity and other 40 students say gain creativity. It means 60% of the students do not improve creativity in this platform. In the digital platform students lack creativity because often students do the question and answer based on the given questions. They do not think beyond that. So, students lack creativity.

The use of polling option creates interest among students. In the graph the result displays that approximately 90 % students say that polling option is very interesting. The polling option creates interest among students because the students get instantly their response through graph and charts. The result related to the use of chart, forum, and instant message in the shows that 90 % of the students say it is more helpful. This is a platform by which students and teacher instantly interact with other. They clear their queries, discuss with each other. This platform makes students to be participatory, attentive and concentrated. Through this teacher supervise students and know whether they are attending the class or not. The graph also presents the result regarding the role of facilitator in the platform that approximately 90% students say that role of facilitator is very effective. Without the facilitator class cannot be taken place. The facilitator schedules the class, supervises, helps, guides, motivates and warns students in the platform. So, the role of the facilitator is very much essential in the platform.

The practice of Reading Comprehension on the platform improves language ability. In the graph finding shows that 85% of the students say that in the platform language ability increases. The platform gives lots of opportunity to practice reading comprehension test. On the platform students do different task like skimming, scanning, jumbled paragraph, note making, summarizing and doing quiz through polling. Through this, students learn different new words and construction of sentences and improve their language ability.

The study fulfills the objective that the Impartus platform improves Reading Comprehension ability. The result shows that 90% students say that through Impartus they improve their Reading Comprehension ability. Regular practice and teacher guidance help students to improve the ability of the Reading Comprehension.

The result also shows that through regular practice in the 90% of the students improve their listening, speaking, reading and writing skill. Students go through different audios, videos links, and online quizzes. All these facilities help students to improve their listening, speaking, reading and writing skills.

The final finding from the survey that the platform is very user friendly and flexible. In the study 80 % of the students say that the platform is user friendly and flexible. Often the absent students also can go through the recorded teaching audio and video files and learn the lessons. Students can attend the classes by staying anywhere. Only students need to have internet connection to attend their classes. In this platform students can ask questions, interact with teacher, share screen, participate in the discussion and can listen the audio and videos files of the teacher repeatedly and these help them to improve their language and communication skills.

CONCLUSION

It is concluded that once a new technology is applied into the classroom, there are some issues for teaching. They are such as difficulty of class management, cognitive overload and distraction. The present study carried out an experiment to investigate the effects of the reading comprehension using the platform. The results indicated that the platform obviously, is a good learning platform from the educational perspective, after completion of appropriate training. If enough time is provided to teachers and students to adapt to the platform then it will be more effective and productive. The finding of study is very much useful for the educators, parents, and policy makers, and provides a theoretical foundation for the popularity use of the platform in educational institution. If the internet connection is good and constant then the platform class becomes effective in teaching and learning process. The common form of assessment in the reading comprehension such as multiple-choice questions and summarization, skimming, scanning and polling in the platform is very user friendly and flexible.

Future study should thus use additional measure methods such as observations and questionnaire. Nonetheless, research study in this area is still in its infancy, and new research paradigm will need to be developed to help researchers and educators to address the advantages and disadvantages in using new technologies for reading texts. It should be noted that the present study has limitations. The findings and their implications discussed in this paper were based on one study with limited sample size, thus further research with larger data samples is recommended for more generalizable results.

REFERENCES

1. Anderson, N. (1999). Exploring second language reading issues and strategies. Washington: Heinle & Heinle Publishers.

2. Grabe, W. (2009). Reading in a second language: Moving from theory and practice. New York: Cambridge University Press.

3. Mangen, A., Walgermo, B. R., & Brønnick, K. (2012). Reading linear texts on paper versus computer screen: Effects on reading comprehension. International Journal of Education Research 58, 61-68. doi:10.1016/ijer202.12.002.

4. Mikulecky, B. (2011). (2nd Ed.) A short course in teaching reading, 2, (39-46). White Plains: Pearson and Longman.

5. McNamara, D. S. (2007). Reading comprehension strategies: Theories, interventions, and technologies (1st ed.). New York: Psychology Press.

6. Polselli, A., & Snow, C. (2003). Rethinking reading comprehension. New York: Guildford Publications, Inc.

7. Supono, L S. (2009). The Effectiveness of Story Grammar Strategy To Improve Students' Reading Comprehension Of Narrative Text. Unpublished thesis, Bandung; University as Pendidikan Indonesia.

8. Saville-Troike, M. (2006). Introducing second language acquisition. New York: Cambridge University Press.

9. Zhang, X., & Cui, G. (2010). Learning perceptions of distance foreign language learners in China: A survey study. System, 38(1), 30-40.

UTOPIA" THE IMMERSIVE REALITY

Mr. Debasish Mohanty
Centurion University of Technology and Management
Odisha, India

INTRODUCTION

A mystical land described by Sir Thomas More's Utopia in 1516 which is said to be the perfect region to reside submerged with harmony. No trace of injustice, where lies no discrimination a land with magic, the desire of achieving perfection has been the cause of countless inventions and infinite theories from the invention of the wheel to the discovery of fire, the construction of the pyramid to the creation of the light bulb, the theory of Pythagoras and the illustration of Leonardo da Vinci humans have always evolved in the quest for perfection, it all took a drastic turn after the creation of the digital world (also known as the Third Industrial Revolution).

The Digital Revolution is the shift from mechanical and analog electronic technology to digital electronics which began in the latter half of the 20th century also gave birth to the device that replicate the human sense accompanied with a display attached for vision, resonating blades for haptic sensation, imitation of smell, and speakers for the sound it was when humans leaped achieving virtual Utopia.

BIRTH OF THE VISION

Stanley Weinbaum Science fiction author penned (Pygmalion's Spectacles) in 1935. In this fiction, the story states the encounter of the main character with a professor who invents a pair of goggles that allow him to visualize movies, sound, taste, smell, and touch from fiction to reality.

PYGMALION'S SPECTACLES

By STANLEY G. WEINBAUM

Author of "The Black Flame," "A Martian Odyssey," etc.

© 1935 by Continental Publications, Inc.

FIGURE 1 Pygmalion's Spectacles

Evolution is a never-ending process as quoted, so do dreams people achieve the vision they dream about if they try hard enough yet the dream of perfection has never escaped from the human portrayal of utopia which years later gave birth to Virtual Reality.

IMITATE REALITY

The creation of the universe

Bible Gateway Genesis 1 - In the beginning, God created the heavens and the earth. Now the earth was formless and empty, darkness was over the surface of the deep, and the Spirit of God was hovering over the waters.

At the dawn of the day of Brahma, this whole universe comes into manifestation from the Unmanifest (Prakrti). When the night begins, it dissolves in that Unmanifest itself.

Gita 8.18

While Myth always believed a supernatural form of celestial being shaped the earth, science always questioned its existence from SuperNova to the collision of meteorites that destroyed all the life forms.

The human desire for perfection and the need for utopia had always made him cross paths with the mystic celestial being or so the creator of the universe, we tend to imitate the creator or reverse engineer its creations.

Humans Desire for Utopia

The Imitation of Reality or to be properly quoted "The Virtual Reality" made us mimic the creation of the celestial being or the biological life form. Virtual reality first came into the picture in 1957 by Morton Heilig. He named it Sensorama and it is considered as one of the earliest forms of Virtual Reality, however, the term Virtual Reality came into picture later in 1987.

VIRTUAL REALITY THE PATH TO PERFECTION

In (1957) "Morton Heilig", a cinematographer, designed the "Sensorama", a theater boxinteractive media gadget that advertised viewers an intuitive experience. The gadget invigorated the users' senses with a seeing screen for locating, wavering wings for touch, gadgets which transmitted smells, and sound.

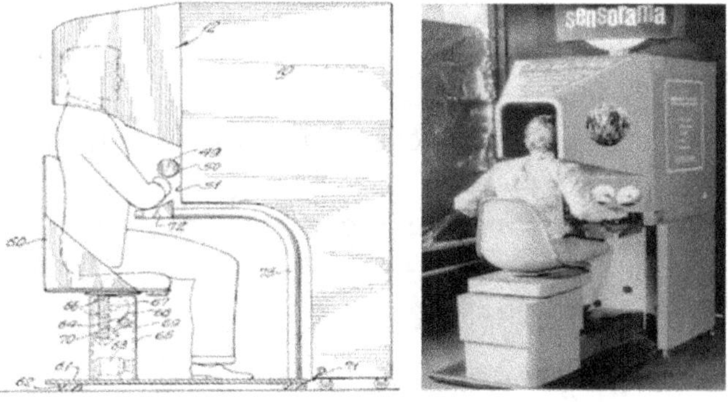

FIGURE 2 Sensorama

In 1961- Comeau and Bryan, two Philco Enterprise engineers, made the primary head-mounted display (HMD) called the Head-sight, it has two display units with a magnet to monitor motion and movement making it the first motion tracking device which allowed users to be in a virtual environment without being physically present at the environment space.

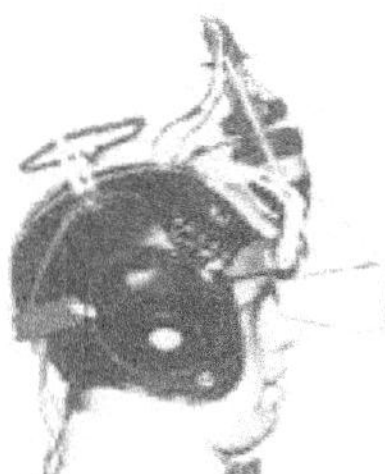

FIGURE 3 HDM

In 1966 a military engineer Thomas Furness, created the primary flight test system for the Air Force. This started a part of intrigued in Virtual Reality median and how it can be utilized for training troops before deploying them at the activity environment.

1968: Ivan Sutherland, a Harvard teacher, and computer researcher concocted the primary VR / AR head-mounted display called 'The Sword of Damocles'. The intimidating contraption was suspended from the ceiling and projected computer-generated design that changed viewpoint as the client moved around.

1978: Made by MIT, the Aspen Movement picture Layout utilized photographs taken from a car in Aspen, Colorado to supply watchers what they called a "Surrogate Travel" involvement. It was a natural first-person see of the city (fundamentally an early VR adjustment of Google Road See re:2007).

1982: The motion picture Tron brought the concept of virtual reality to the masses. Adapted by gamers, the characters were submerged in a completely virtual environment that reenacted a video game.

FIGURE 3 Tron

1986: Furness worked on his Discuss Drive recreation extending through the 80s and within the conclusion created the Outwardly Coupled Airborne Systems Test system (VCASS). The framework gave pilots a virtual view that streamlined the torrent of data they get each moment.

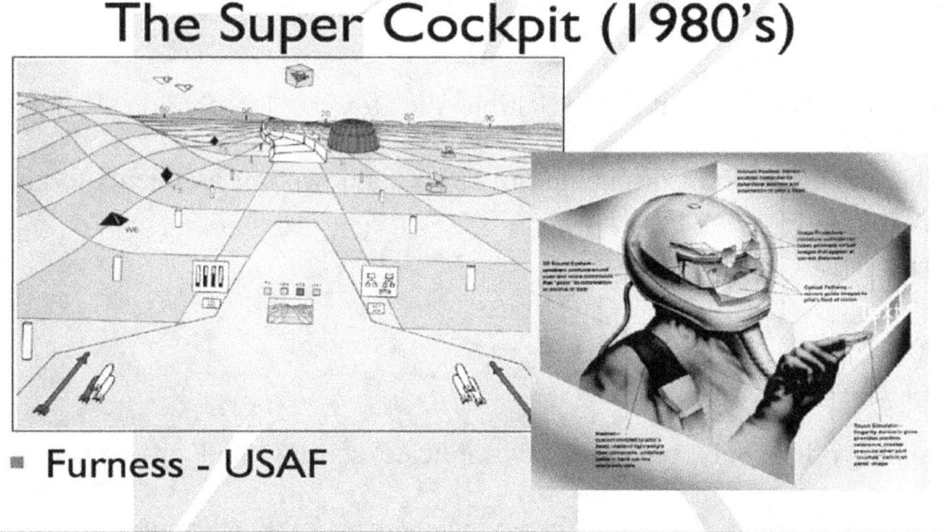

Furness, T. A. (1986, September). The super cockpit and its human factors challenges. In *Proceedings of the Human Factors and Ergonomics Society Annual Meeting* (Vol. 30, No. 1, pp. 48-52). SAGE Publications.

FIGURE 4 Super Cockpit

Georgia Tech and Emory College analysts in 1997 joined to make war zone simulation for the veterans suffering from Post-traumatic disorder which was an aid in reducing the mental trauma by simulating virtual war zone.

In 2007 Google introduced its Google Street view which acted as a visual site of the mapped area by simulating 360 panoramic view of the particular area this was captured with a camera mounted over a moving car to project street, interior and buildings.

VR TODAY

Within the final decade, the world of virtual reality has made enormous enhancements, for the most part from the tech giants' fight that followed – Amazon, Apple, Facebook, Google, Microsoft, Sony, and Samsung all built VR and AR divisions. In any case, buyers are still on the fence about VR Tech because it tends to come with a strong cost tag attached.

2013: Valve enterprise found a way to show lag-free VR substance and shared it unreservedly with Oculus and other vendors. Valve and HTC declared their association nearby the HTC Vive headset and controllers in 2015 and discharged the primary adaptation in 2016.

2014: Sony reveals Venture Morpheus, aka PlayStation VR, for the PlayStation 4 video amusement console. The last buyer form discharged in 2016, empowering its clients to not fair play the amusement, but "live the game".

THE SCIENTIFIC BASICS OF VIRTUAL REALITY

At its heart, VR technology has only one goal: to replicate settings and environments accurately enough to trick the human brain into believing them as reality. From a science point of view, that all begins by understanding how our brains perceive the objects we see to create a mental image of the world around us.

Without going into too much detail, the easiest reason is that our understanding of reality is based on laws that we create using our experience as a reference. For example, when we see the sky, it tells us the direction "higher" is heading. If we see objects that we can recognize, we can use their size compared to each other to judge the space. We can also detect light sources by collecting the shadows cast by the objects around us. VR programmers may use these traditional rules to create simulated worlds that fulfill our mental standards of reality. The effect, when they do, is a smooth experience that we perceive as "true."

FULLY-IMMERSIVE REALITY SOLUTION

With an addition of haptic sensors to existing head mounded display and standalone display and projection device embedded with harness, body armor and gloves it provides the user a filly immersive experience.

This particular device or solution is used for VR games, arcade and training or even in your home (empty, non-fragile space recommended).

FIGURE 4 Immersive Experience

Completely interactive simulations give users the most authentic experience possible, complete with sight and sound. With a wide field of view, the VR headsets provide high-resolution content. You will feel like you are there, whether you are traveling or battling the bad guys.

SEMI-IMMERSIVE VIRTUAL REALITY SIMULATIONS

Semi-immersive experiences provide users with a partially virtual environment to interact with. This type of virtual reality experience is generally used for education and training for students and trainees to simulate the real-world virtual challenges and situations generally by a large motion display while the user is still being in the physical environment which results in reducing human errors.

FIGURE 5 Semi-immersive experiences

TO FUTURE AND BEYOND

"What's Next?" it will always be unpredicted some events may be magical some might create wonders

Immersive virtual reality has barely cleared the launch pad, while a new technology which was coined as Full Dive Virtual Reality where the brain is stimulated to be in the virtual space instead of just creating a visual illusion by a display and a pair of convex lenses the theory is proposed to divert the brain waves by electromagnetic fields transmitted through the hardware to the neuron receptor of human receptor nerves.

Yes, advances are being made across a wide range of technologies that will allow users to control computers with a mere thought, but when can we consider the full-immersive technology to be the next big change? We might not be too far away to fly as shazam or to control virtual magic

HUMBLE BEGINNING

In 2013, Harvard University conducted a human- brain-to-mouse-brain experiment. In the procedure the human brain waves were captured and converted into digital signals which can further be called as electromagnetic wave signals the one responsible for brain function, in this particular experiment researchers were able to manipulate the brain functions of another multicellular organism, the test subject was a rat whose tail movement was controlled using the experiment the test was carried out as brain to brain communication, later in 2015 the university of California conducted a similar experiment with human brain replicating the effect of experiment conducted by Harvard University in which they were unsuccessful in controlling the mouse tail but were able to help a paraplegic man to walk for 4 meters with the help of EEG device and software.

WORTH IT?

Full dive virtual reality development isn't all fun and games. It might be just in theory with a few recent advancements by CEO of Tesla and SpaceX Elon Musk who proposed the full dive gear which would enable users to merge into the simulation itself making it the first of its kind, maybe we have to wait for few more years to witness the technology as constant work and effort have been added to deliver for its development, concerning the movie "READY PLAYER ONE" and Japanese animated series "SAO" the nerve gear might just be real.

We were able to configure or to keep it simple mimicked the creation of the creator by simulating animation into a virtual human being and also created the so-called virtual Utopia where everyone can be whatever they desire: small, tall, good looking, beast, bird, or mermaid.

No death or disease a world is floating with magic but when the reality is removed all that is left would be virtual keeping it simple "lies", the reality is hard and cruel and sometimes unfair but at the same time it is our reality and we have to accept it, so the question remains is it worth it? I will just leave it here, that's upon the reader to answer.

REFERENCES

1. Aviram Eisenberg FDVR. Adapted from

2. https://www.researchgate.net/publication/271667415_Construction_safety_training_using_immersive_virtual_reality>   <https://appreal-vr.com/blog/full-dive-virtual-reality-how-it-works/comment-page-1/>

3. Sir Thomas More's Utopia (1516)

4. Bridget Poetker, What Is Virtual Reality? From https://learn.g2.com/virtual-reality

TECHNOLOGY-ORIENTED LEARNING OPEN BROADCASTER SOFTWARE

Dr. Mohammad Aamir Pasha
Assistant Professor
Centurion University of Technology and Management
Odisha, India

INTRODUCTION

Technology-oriented learning, which belongs to the online or web-based learning, is students centric teaching and learning style which consists of digital content and also computer mediated communication. Learning through technology or with the help of Internet or intranets, through broadcast, video conferencing, chat rooms and webcast. These all belong to the Technology-oriented Learning (TOL). In this pandemic situation, most important concern is how we can conduct classes and how we continue teaching and learning process. In India there is high rate of digital illiteracy and digital divide. In this era where Indian society shifts from classroom teaching to online teaching the biggest problem is how it has become user friendly and easy to access. The utility of learning technology has extended over past decades, it also intensively increases in this pandemic situation; even if there are severe usability issues that cause positive and negative effects on the learning experience. This also emerges in many available technologies.

Technology acts as a catalyst for enhancing educational productivity. It is also bringing changes in the basic structure of deliberation. It also works as a source for both teaching and learning, technology allows in the study room with technology-oriented learning tools, such as computers and other digital devices. It is also help for the increases course structure, practices, other study materials, learning duration 24 into 7 days in a week, student involvement and learning and understanding capacity. Technology-oriented learning has influence force to change teaching model. This new model connects teacher to students with professional resources, content and technological system to enhance learning and teaching.

In the last few months, the distinction between technical users and non-users in the society has been made even more clear. We can say this gap between two parts of society as digital divide. These days many online learning and technology-oriented learning software are emerging. Open Broadcaster Software (OBS) is also one of them. In this chapter discuss how OBS will helpful in TOL.

This chapter has analysed how OBS and other Technology-oriented learning software work and how it is helpful for the teacher and students. The study consists of online education process especially Open Broadcaster Software and how it is different from other software which is helpful for the online teaching and learning process and technology-oriented learning. This chapter also emphasizes how digital divide and digital media literacy is needed for online education. This paper totally depends upon secondary sources and personal interview. The main emphasis on this paper to explore how to OBS is different from other live streaming software. In this chapter also we discuss how this OBS is playing the role of accentuating the technology-oriented learning.

TECHNOLOGY-ORIENTED LEARNING

The present pandemic has not only affected economies across the world but also rattled political structures and governments. While some countries face stagnation in growth and serious health security issues, almost all face challenges to their education systems.

It can be divided into two types:

1. Online Classroom

2. Smart Classroom

Online classroom refers to web-based classes which are used as an all-time accessible content through the various website and web-based platform. Smart Classroom can be seen as a conventional classroom teaching method but totally technology-oriented.

Here are some ideas in which we can adopt technology-oriented learning tactics:

- Question-based Learning

Question-based learning is more helpful for the development of understanding. Use of assessment or assignment learning this approach is to help full for the development of competency. It can also include question solving and basics of lesson understanding. This is a mostly student-centric method or approaches and totally depends upon the project, assignment, inquiry and problem-oriented. This style of learning develops students critical thinking at a global level.

- Student-centric Content

In this approach, students can create and design the content that can be shared in the school, online teaching platforms and learning management system. This type of learning approaches is now available on the web. Students can create the content and they can also provide different opinion on which they learned.

- Collaborative learning

This is totally technology-based and web-based learning style. In the technology-oriented learning time, we can access content every time and anywhere with different content and beyond the borders.

- Competency or Capability-based education

This approach is developed with the help of technology-based; the main focus of this approach is effective learning, not time-based learning. In this approach, students will use either e-content platform or in-person teaching to understand effectively.

In this section, the quality is maintained while the target group or audience is not able to take the information. With the loosing of the bond between location and time the tension is reduced and learning become more effective after occur. Another learning approach that will develop through technology is competency-based education. This alternative approach aims to focus on effective learning, rather than time-based learning.

- Active learning

Active-learning / Hands-on learning means students learn from self-experience and try to help each other with the help of learning methods. In this method, students support each other and they give space to consider their own opinion. The teacher plays a role is only as a guide, not an instructor, the teacher will help only when they need to act or respond when any hurdle occurs.

- Blended learning

Combination of both classroom method, online and traditional classroom method refer as blended learning. Mentor and students both combine join physical classroom and students can access study material and classwork to be complete on digital form. This model of learning also gives a facility to learning at home with digital device.

- Flipped learning

It is a kind of blended method of learning but it is just an opposite to conventional method or conventional teaching approach. In this method students use all time available content on digital platform i.e. students can access content like videos and other material at home and they can discuss in details in the classroom. In simple word students can access content or information, in-home and task will be done in the classroom (Kruse, 2020).

DIFFERENT SOFTWARE FOR TEACHING AND LEARNING

There is a lot of software that is in the market for live streaming, screen sharing, for classroom teaching and video and audio creation.

- Streamlabs OBS
- XSplit
- Wirecast
- vMix
- Nvidia Shadowplay
- Lightstream

This all software is useful for the live streaming and video recording feature. Many people are used as live streaming and live online classes with the different platform with the same content at the same time. OBS is also online broadcaster software which gives more option i.e. video recording, live streaming, slide share and video converter option.

DIGITAL DIVIDE IN INDIA

During the lockdown in India, the education sector has highlighted the status of the digital divide in India. NSO data is also revealed that the rural and urban digital user gap.

The difference between an immature and mature user of digital technologies can be denoted as the digital divide, in refining word we can say that gap between access of digital device or content and the people who do not do not use the digital devices. It can be denoted age-wise, gender, economic background, geographical and educational criteria.

India has a big gap between digital technology user and non-user. It is the main concern and hurdle of the technology-oriented learning platform.

TABLE 1: Percentage of person of age 5 years and above who are able to operate computer, able to use internet and used internet

persons of age 5 years and above	percentage		
			Rural
	male	female	person
able to operate a computer	12.6	7.0	9.9
able to use internet	17.1	8.5	13.0
used internet during last 30 days	14.6	6.6	10.8
			Urban
able to operate a computer	37.5	26.9	32.4
able to use internet	43.5	30.1	37.1
used internet during last 30 days	40.4	26.6	33.8
			Rural + Urban
able to operate a computer	20.0	12.8	16.5
able to use internet	25.0	14.9	20.1
used internet during last 30 days	22.3	12.5	17.6

Source: NSSO 75th Round 2017-2018.

According to the 75th round of National Sample Survey conducted between July 2017 and June 2018, just 9.9 per cent of rural people able to operate a computer, and 13 per cent of people were able to use the internet, The situation of the urban area has not reached half of the population, only 32.4, 37.1 and 33.8 per cent of people can able to operate a computer, use of the internet and use of the internet during last 30 days respectively.

This data is also shrunken when we analyze combinedly rural and urban area both. Only 16.5 percent of the population able to operate a computer and 20.1 percent of the population can access to the internet. Its shows huge difference between users and non-users. And this situation has emerged in publicly during the lockdown.

ONLINE BROADCAST SOFTWARE FOR TEACHING AND LEARNING PROCESS

Open Broadcaster Software (OBS) is a totally free of cost OBS is also open-source software, it has also given the facility of cross-platform streaming with recording program. It means in this software; we can use the combination of the video and audio from different sources. In another word we can say that this software gives us facility to connect between large number of channels and gives option to combine with flexibility of computer-based content. It's also called Software Vision Mixer. This software gives us combine option of audio and visual content in the single platform.

OBS started as a project which has been created by Hugh Jim Baily; after that it developed quickly with the collaboration of many online forms. but quickly grew with the help of many online collaborators working both to improve OBS and spread the knowledge about the program.

OBS is the free access or open access software, it is very helpful for low budget live streaming. It gives us all option which is needed to create a good live broadcast. This software can't be compared with paid professional software.

OBS is open source free software and it gives a lot of create content option i.e. live streaming, screen recording, real time screen sharing, devise capture, recording and broadcasting. Its also give a facility to many pre-sets for live streaming like YouTube and other social networking sites.

The user interface of OBS divided in five parts:

- Scenes

- Audio Mixer

- Transition

- Controls Panel

- Sources

This software gives us a lot of options like switch the mode or source i.e. you can change your source link like live to recorded screen and recorded content to slide share. It gives hotkey option for change to one mode to another mode. The control panel or hotkey gives the options to start, stop and pause button for adjusting video content in live streaming. We can also control audio streaming through the self-assigned key. In the studio mode it gives two screen preview, there is lot of tutorial available online which gives some idea on how to use OBS for teachers and students.

CONCLUSION

Technology gives us a lot of options for the development of not only content but also teaching and learning methods, for example, it gives us a new experiment in teaching and learning style, easy way of creating content, intersection in worldwide level, understanding ability to new information and access to information to a large extent. The conventional method of learning does not change due to technology, it is just supported by the verity of learning approaches as a new method of learning. Development is needed for new changes in education, as a skilled and a knowledgeable workforce work as a catalyst for economic growth. Nowadays, for the development, it is required for changes in production processes and training for the new profession.

The most important part of OBS is live streaming and recording, with preview part, screen recording and slide share facility it creates like the professional output. OBS gives the broad option and professional environment for video broadcasting, recording and web streaming.

OBS can be helpful for the courses which are delivered through web-based, it is specifically designed online course like, slide share of study material, an instructional video for the course, audio recordings of lectures, sort videos and course material.

REFERENCE:

1. Kidd, Terry. & Lonnie R. Morris, Jr. 2017. *Handbook of Research on Instructional Systems and Educational Technology*. PA: IGI Global Publication.

2. Kruse, Finja 2020. *8 Ways to Embrace Technology-Based Learning Approaches*. Retrieve From: https://www.skillsyouneed.com/rhubarb/technology-based-learning-approaches.html

3. Deschaine, Mark; Whale, David. 2017. *Increasing Student Engagement in Online Educational Leadership Courses*. Journal of Educators Online: 6.

4. Chernova, Marta. 2020. *Best live streaming software [Updated for 2019]*. Retrieve From: https://www.epiphan.com/blog/best-streaming-software-2019/#streamlabs

5. Robert C. Wicklein and Jay W. Rojewski. 1995. *The Relationship Between Psychological Type and Professional Orientation Among Technology Education Teachers*. Journal of Technology Education Vol. 7 No. 1.

6. Chen Annie. 2018. *Psychology behind the reliance of technology. The Campanile*. Retrieve From: https://thecampanile.org/2018/09/23/psychology-behind-the-reliance-of-technology/

7. Psu Lecture Notes. 2017. *Applied Social Psychology*. Retrieve From: https://sites.psu.edu/aspsy/2017/10/30/technology-in-the-classrooms/

8. Bandura, A. 1986. *Social Foundations of Thought and Action: A Social Cognitive Theory*. Upper Saddle River, NJ: Prentice Hall.

9. Kowalski, K. 2016. *When Smartphones go to School*. Science News for Students.

10. Digital pedagogy. 2020. Wikipedia. Retrieve From:

    https://en.wikipedia.org/wiki/Digital_pedagogy#:~:text=Digital%20pedagogy%20is%20the%20study,in%20the%20theory%20of%20constructivism.

11. Rousseau, Paulina. 2020. What is Digital Pedagogy? Retrieve From:

    https://guides.library.utoronto.ca/digitalpedagogy

12. Open Broadcaster Software Studio (Multiplatform) Help Guide. 2016. Retrieve From:

    https://obsproject.com/forum/resources/open-broadcaster-software-studio-multiplatform-help-guide-pdf.365/

13. Pandey, Kundan. 2020. COVID-19 lockdown highlights India's great digital divide. Down to Earth. Retrieve From:

    https://www.downtoearth.org.in/news/governance/covid-19-lockdown-highlights-india-s-great-digital-divide-72514

ADOBE SPARK:
AN AID TO ONLINE TEACHING AND LEARNING PLATFORM

Ms. Suchismita Nayak
Lecturer
Centurion University of Technology and Management
Odisha,India

INTRODUCTION

Comprehensive changes have been observed in recent times, in the conventional method of education. Physical presence of both educators and students is no longer an option in the learning process. According to the changes in the educational perspective, educators always come forward, accept and calibrate with the variations and enfold the idea of online education which has become the spearhead in imparting education. At the present period of time, quality education can be accessed easily at whatever time the learner urge for in this era of online education. In this online teaching and learning process, number of tools are being developed by various application developers and being used by the educators and educational organisations to overcome various challenges in the domain of education. The value of internet has increased over the decade. In the education world also, the demand has increased its peak. Due to the increase in demand for the online education and taking into account various factors it has become very much essential for all to use and learn astounding mobile and web app known as Adobe Spark. This application acts as an aid to enhance the performance of the educators for providing effective online teaching to support and assist students to perform better.

This chapter speaks about Adobe Spark, an integrated suite of media creation applications for mobile and web developed by Adobe Systems, which acts as an aid to online teaching platform. This application works as an accessibility enhancer for educators in the online teaching environment resulting in efficacious online teaching practices, at the same time enhancing student and educator performance. The employment of the tools oof Adobe Spark can bring productive outcomes in online teaching and learning practices in the form of Spark Page, Spark Post, and Spark Video and can enhance student satisfaction and retention. Creation of Spark pages and Spark videos by educators will work as a resource to escort and guide a student with the simplest impactful visual stories and with spectacular social graphics.

SETTING THE CONTEXT

Now a days it has become very essential to be more creative and use the skill to be in the race of this digital age. As creativity is in progress, IT and creative software with internet are in great demand. Adobe Spark is considered as an important tool that helps every individual to be more creative. It is one such web and mobile based application which is used to create videos, graphics and websites. Adobe Spark is considered as one of the best online software which is available free of cost to the users and is super easy to use for creation of web stories, graphics and videos. It converts the teaching materials to be very attractive and interesting, and likely to get positive response from the students, reducing the chance of distraction.

Digital literacy is the skill we need to learn, work and survive in this digital era to have access to information for smooth flow of communication through online digital platforms to social media and mobile devices. It focuses on the potentiality to employ, locate and design information online in a favourable and applicable way. Adobe Spark is the app which makes the flow of communication simple and alluring. It is a cross functional design app which can be used by multi-disciplinary educators to create and design the contents required to deliver the students to have better understanding and enhance their performance level. It has been designed in such a way that everyone can have access to it by simply creating a user account and login to the account to create web stories and animated videos by using various features at any time and can be accessed anywhere.

ADOBE SPARK: AS A TEACHING AND LEARNING PLATFORM

Multimedia is a comprehensive term consisting of various media formats. The combination of text, images, animation, video and interactivity outcome is multimedia. In this 21st century educational multimedia application demand has increased and are being used to ameliorate teaching and learning efficacy. Using multimedia for educational domain necessitates various components to ensure that teaching and learning process is on flow. Before it was very expensive to create admirable videos, images and audios for designing purpose. But the observation says, now we have high definition software applications which provides a huge support to create multimedia projects with uncomplication and unchallenging. It is observed that the student and educator interaction is increasing with the progress in the teaching and learning process with the help of multimedia applications.

Adobe Spark an online mobile and web design application, which can be used for providing visual aid by the educators to create and shape the lessons to appear more fascinating and influence the students gain or acquire knowledge with the process educators impart education. Adobe Spark consists of three tools namely Spark Post, Spark Page and Spark Video which are very simple and easy to create prepossessing visual contents. These tools substantiate to be beneficial for the educators to create Spark page and Spark video for the students having clear and precise picture of the contents they have in their syllabus, at the same time fringe benefit to the students for having better understanding of the subject matter by the help of these digital story telling tools.

Adobe Spark can be considered as an aid for teaching and learning process. Educators can use this free design tools to create meaningful captivating glides and videos for the students and helping them to understand the subject matter. As this app is fun and interesting, students can also create glide shows for the presentation purpose and represent their thoughts and ideas related to the topics concerned with the help of this user friendly app and use the wonderful features available free of cost to showcase their skills and the depth of knowledge they possess in a particular subject matter. As this app can be accessed from any device, so it becomes easier for the educators to create web stories using the glides show and videos and then share the same with the students through social media and emails. the students can also share their presentations through social media and emails also. The features of the tools enable the educators to design the videos and web pages in such a manner that the students can easily comprehend the subject matter with great inquisitiveness. Adobe Spark is not only beneficial for the students in the field of gaining knowledge and education but also at the same time educate the educators to use their own creative skills for developing aesthetical contents with the help of the tools and features it provides and these contents later proves to be rewarding for the students to enhance their knowledge in the particular subject matter or related topics and excel in their career prospects.

ADOBE SPARK TOOLS AND ITS BENEFITS

Adobe Spark cater its users with three magnificent tools named as Spark Post, Spark Page and Spark Video which can be used to explore and design the creativity to accomplish the task.

- **Spark Post**

With the help of Spark Post, impressive and captivating graphics can be created or designed by the users by using the attractive designs and themes available. Adobe Spark comes with different size of canvas for digital graphic needs for various purposes. No graphic design skills are required to design a graphic for any purpose. It is a free online app which can be easily used to edit pictures and apply text, filters as well as adjust contrast, brightness, saturation, warmth, or sharpness—all with a few taps. The graphics created by using the Spark Post can be used in the Spark Pages and Spark Videos. This tool can be used by the students to design posters for presentation based on various topics and invitations by implementing their creative ideas and the various free features available to them through this app. Spark Post enable the students to add multiple images in one graphic to narrate a topic.This activity of creating graphics by Spark Post can enhance the skill and can prove to be beneficial for the learner in the near future.

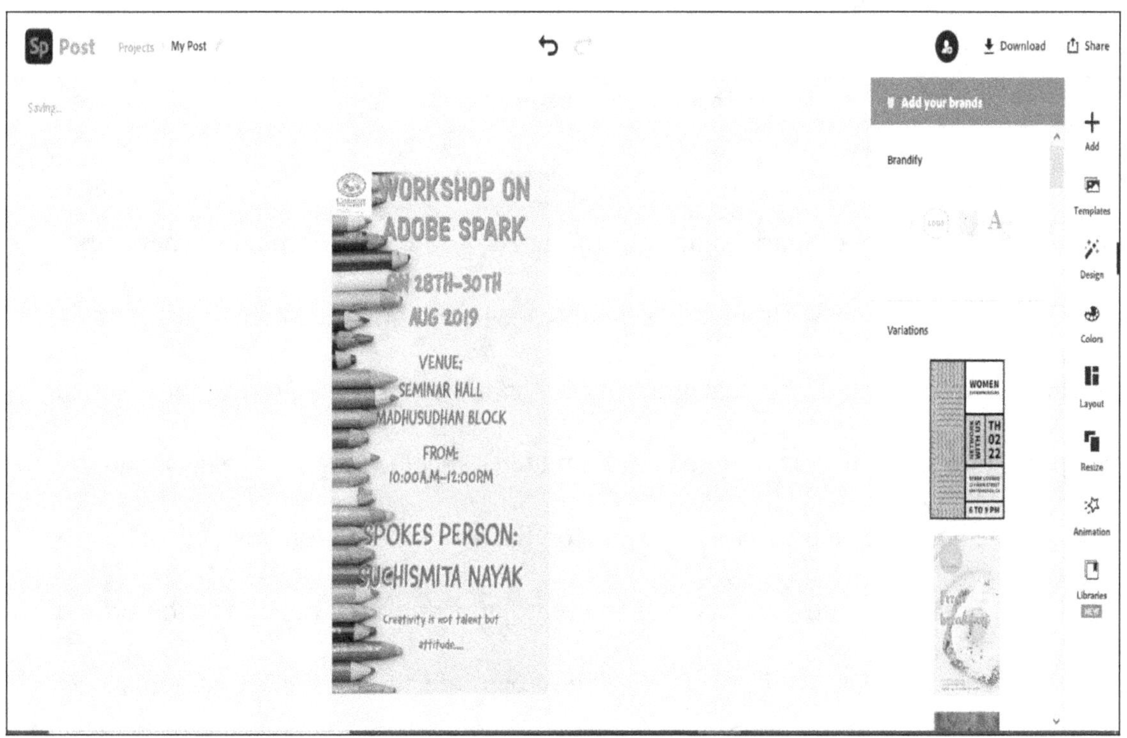

FIGURE 1: Spark Post (Screen Shot)

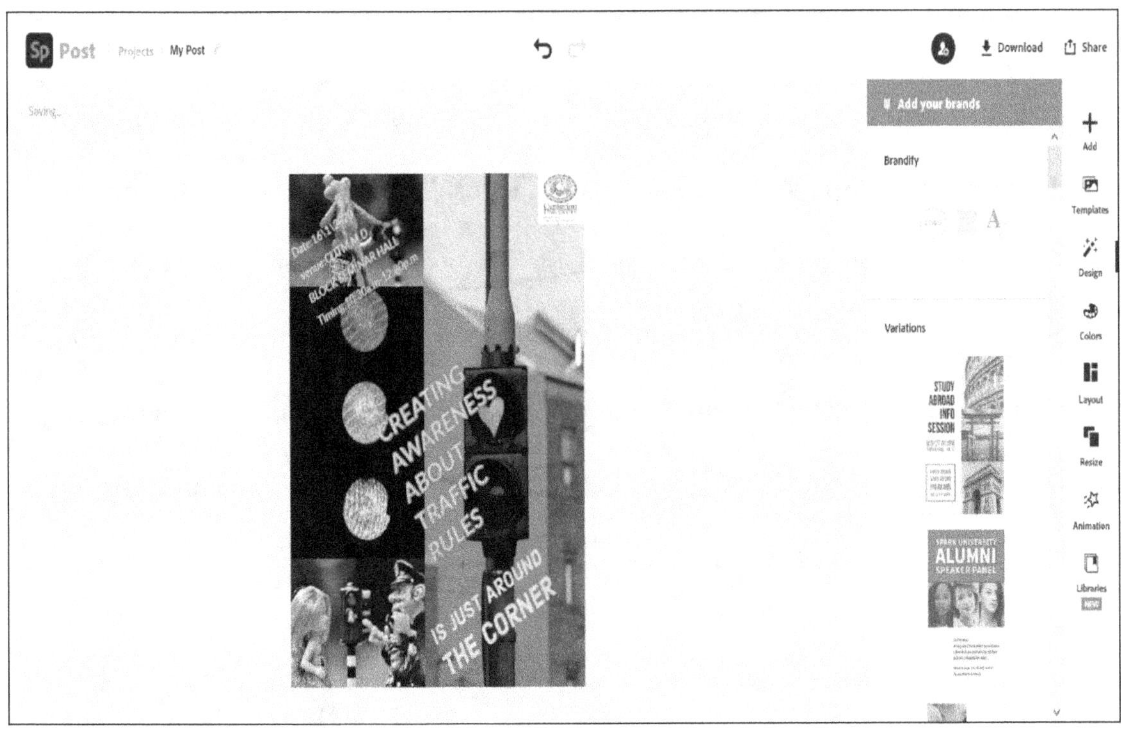

FIGURE 2: Spark Post (Screen Shot)

● Spark Page

This is a tool provided by Adobe Spark, that help the users to create web pages where text, images and videos can be added with all other features when required. Web pages can be used for presentation purposes. Here research papers can be turned into digital stories, visually enthralling journal can be designed and created, spectacular web pages can be created with a cause and glide shows can be used for the smooth motion instead of using standard page scroll. Educators can use this tool to create amazing web pages for the online learning purpose for the students. In the web page they can add text, images and videos by using the theme available and can set the content into motion by using the Glide show. Spark Page can be of great help for the educators, to create contents which proves to be beneficial for the students to understand the subject matter in a more colourful pictorial form, with attractive theme and fonts which drag the attention of the students for a longer time period and have great impact in their learning process.

FIGURE 3: Spark Page (Screen Shot)

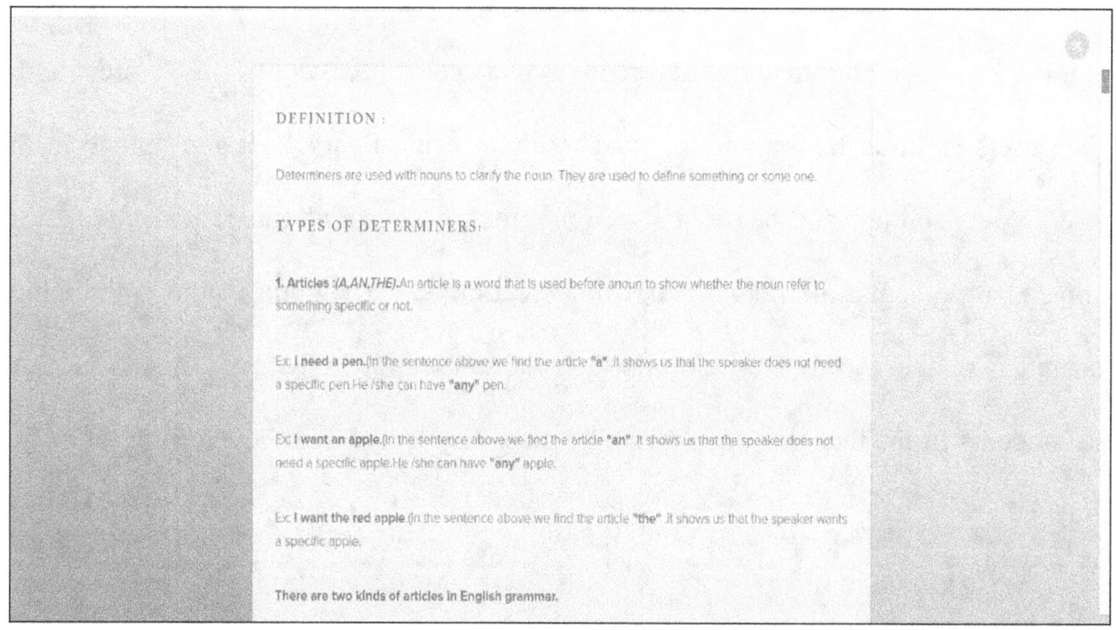

FIGURE 4: Spark Page (Screen Shot)

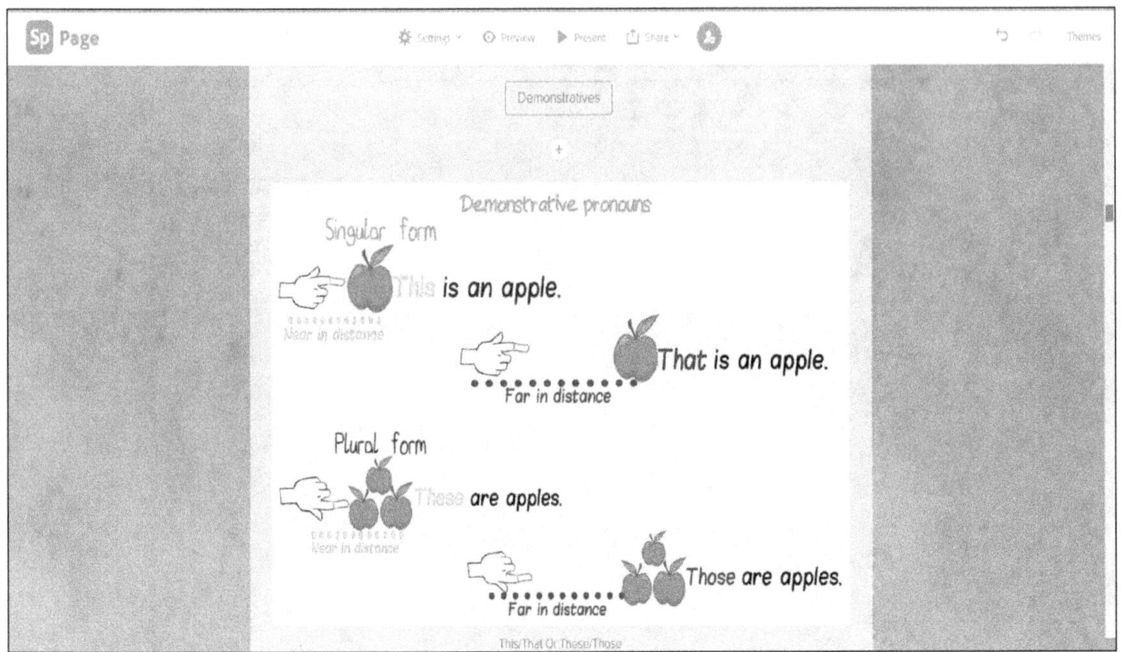

FIGURE 5: Spark Page (Screen Shot)

- **Spark Video**

Spark is the best option for modernised, trim and elegant videos which can be created by the users. As this tool is available free of cost, the users can use their creative skills to prepare the videos. The users can use the graphics created by them using Spark Post and upload in the videos, use layouts and present themes and colours, text, background music with the feature of recording own voice narration as required for creation and designing of the video which can be shared with the world. This tool also proves to be more effective for educators to attract the students in the teaching and learning process by increasing the learning outcomes of the students.

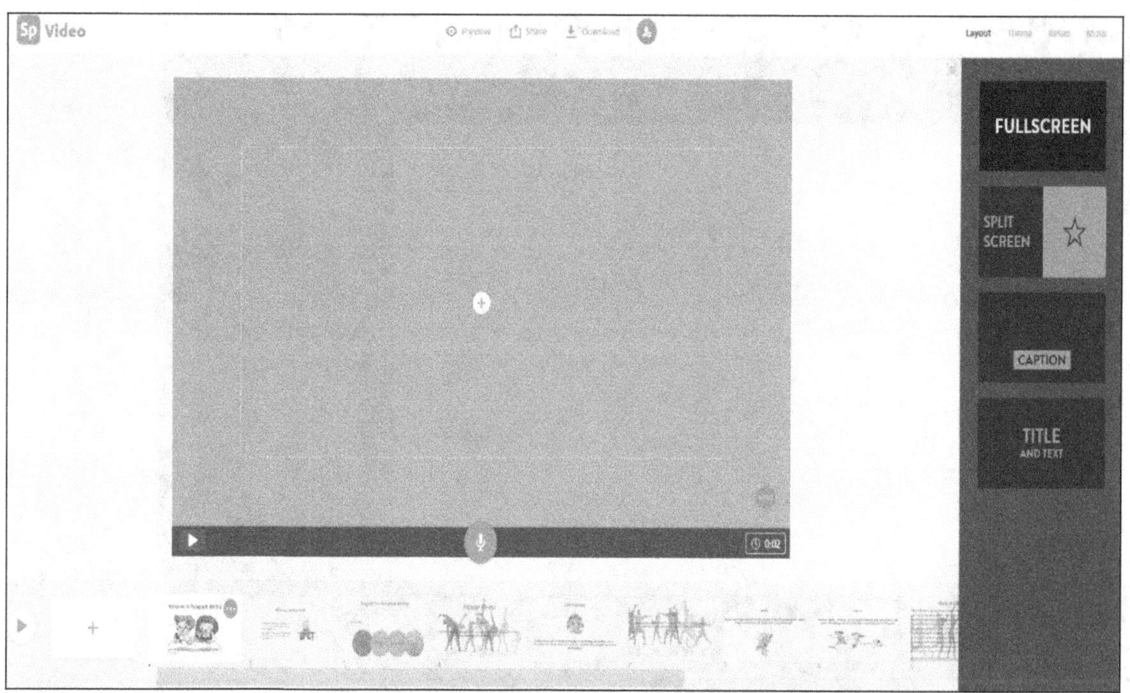

FIGURE 6: Spark Video Layout (Screen Shot)

FIGURE 7: Spark Video (Screen Shot)

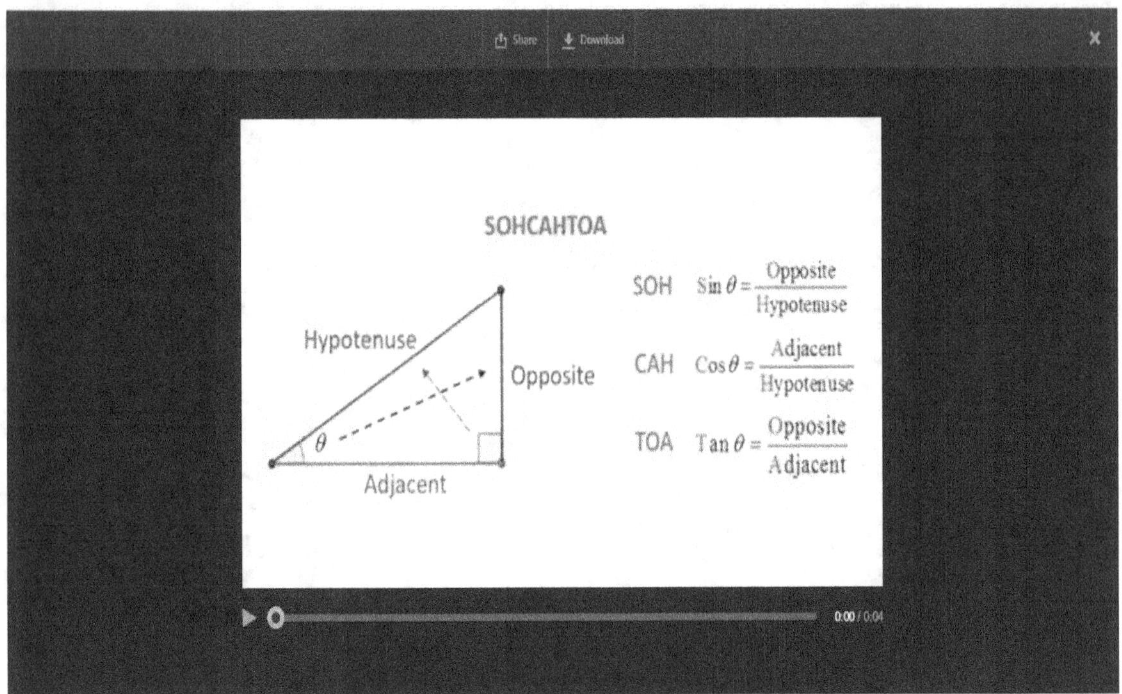

FIGURE 8: Spark Video (Screen Shot)

ATTRIBUTES OF ADOBE SPARK

The effectiveness of Spark tools depends on the characteristics given below:

Captivating Typography

To make a text more effective good typography is very much essential to use it as visual to convey the message and entices the attention of the viewer and to keep them engaged with the text. Adobe Spark is one such application which has collection of free fonts professionally designed and can be used for various purposes. Specially creating social graphics, web pages and videos of short length. Spark Post Typography is a well-built wonderful design tool that uses letters and characters as a means of artistry to send an ineffaceable message to the audience. This signifies that by the employment of distinct selective fonts, using letters in an awe-inspiring way to design or create them into a work of art, and pleasing and appealing to the senses of the audience is possible through this feature.

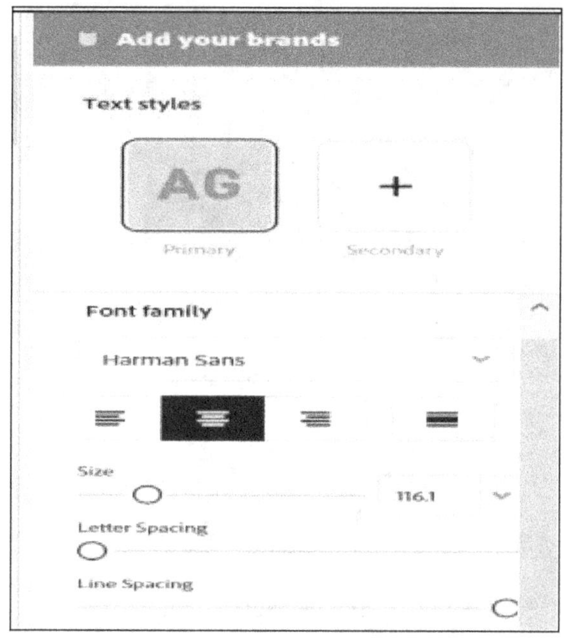

FIGURE 9: Customizable Fonts (Screen Shot)

Iconic Depiction

Adobe Spark allows its users to pick any iconic image from thousands of images on web and also allow the users to select their personal collections on Google Photos, Adobe Creative Cloud and Lightroom CC. This feature enables the users to design the Spark Post, Spark Page and Spark Video more fascinating so that it can be instantly communicated, as pictures are more suitable for communication and can be easily understood. The users can use this feature to upload images into the workspace and also have the option of exploring Spark's free photos from Unsplash, where the user can find a large collection of images which can be selected and uploaded in the workspace to cater the need of designing so that the user can escort the masterly sight to existent.

FIGURE 10: Images (Screen Shot)

Executive Themes

Layout is an exhibition of plan or design in which the user put out the components on a page. Adobe Spark provide its users to explore wide variety of best-in-class layouts for Spark Post, Videos and Pages with an impactful fusion of colour and font. The purpose of layout is to convey the message correctly and to showcase information in a systematic way making the important elements stand out.

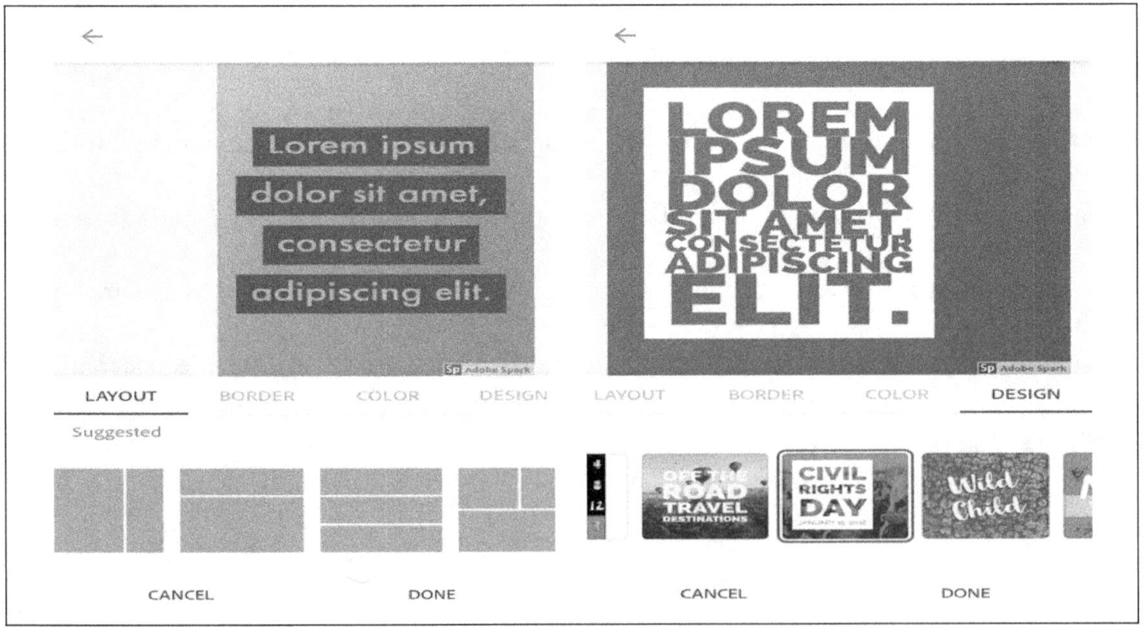

FIGURE 11: Adobe Spark Layouts(Screen Shot)

Design Templates

In Adobe Spark, there are collection of free executive templates. The designer templates draw up the design process simple and uncomplicated. Social graphics and videos can be easily designed within a very short time without any knowledge of design skill. The users can use this feature and create the required contents or simply they can design their own templates by making it more captivating for the viewer with required amount of information as well.

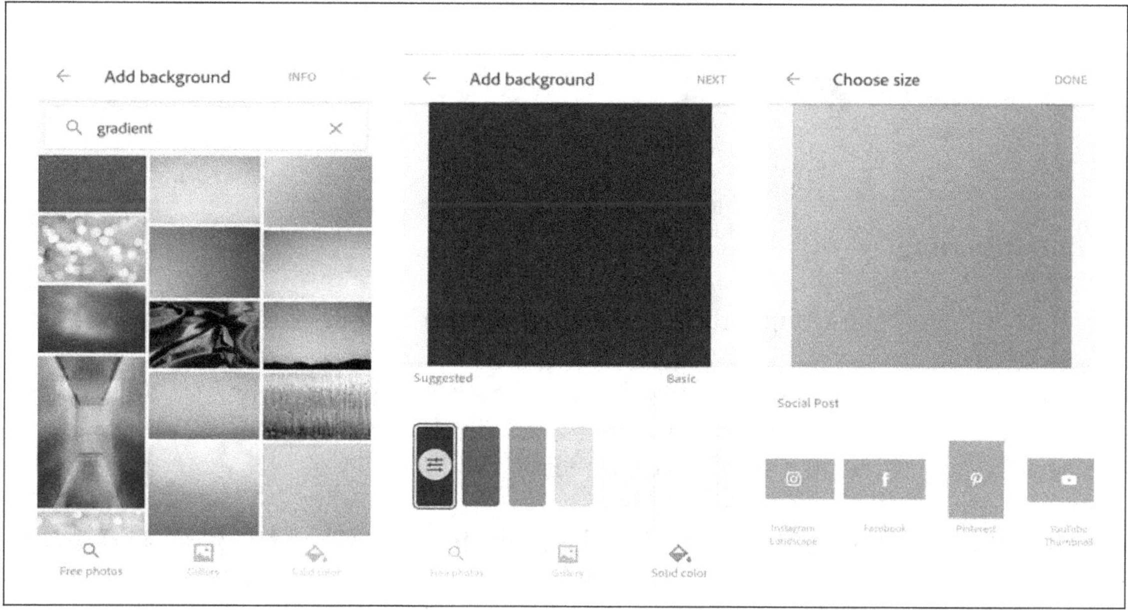

FIGURE 12: Background Theme(Screen Shot)

Customizable Colour

It is one the feature which is provided by Adobe Spark taking into account the particular needs of the users. Customization allows an individual to modify the colours while creating beautiful graphics, web pages and video stories and are capable of attracting and holding interest of the audience towards the project.

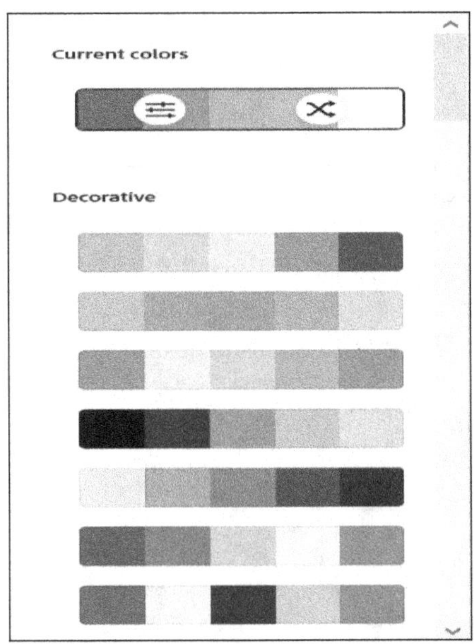

FIGURE 13: Colour Palettes (Screen Shot)

Customizable Branding

This feature of Adobe Spark supports the users to create brand. The user can build a customized logo to cater the required purpose. Adobe Spark offers logo templates and layouts which can be modified as per the user's requirement. The logo designed by the user can be used in their graphics, and videos to personalise the projects.

FIGURE 14: Customized Logo creation (Screen Shot)

FIGURE 15: Customized Logo(Screen Shot)

Cross Device Sync

The users can sync their designs across different devices by the help of Adobe Spark. This feature helps the users to sync between desktops, laptops and with mobile devices. It means the user can start work in a mobile device, after that he/she can carry on the work with his/her web browser, and then can further edit the work on their mobile, and continue.

Save and Share

Adobe Spark help the users to save their designed graphics, web pages and videos in the device. Even if the creation is not saved by the user, Spark saves all the designs automatically for the user in the Project folder which can be accessed easily. One of the significant traits of Adobe Spark is that from any device with online access it can be accessed. This accessibility enables the user to share the designed contents with relative ease, through social media and emails to the receivers or viewers worldwide. This feature helps the educators to share the required subject matter created by them by using Adobe Spark tools, where the students can easily access and visualise and understand the topic or the subject matter shared by the educators.

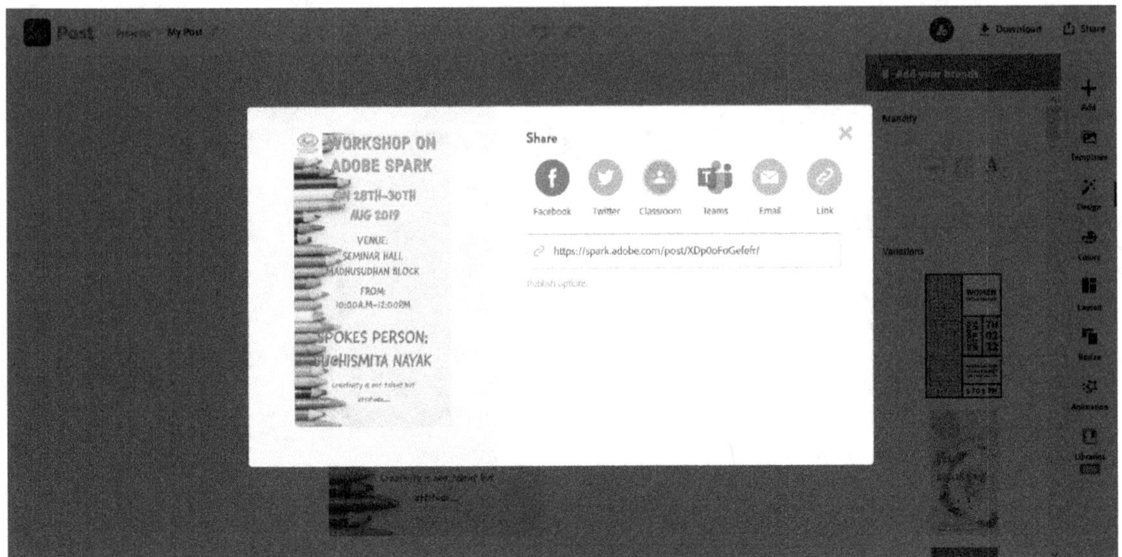

FIGURE 16: Spark Post sharing options(Screen Shot)

FIGURE 17: Spark Post creating link for sharing (Screen Shot)

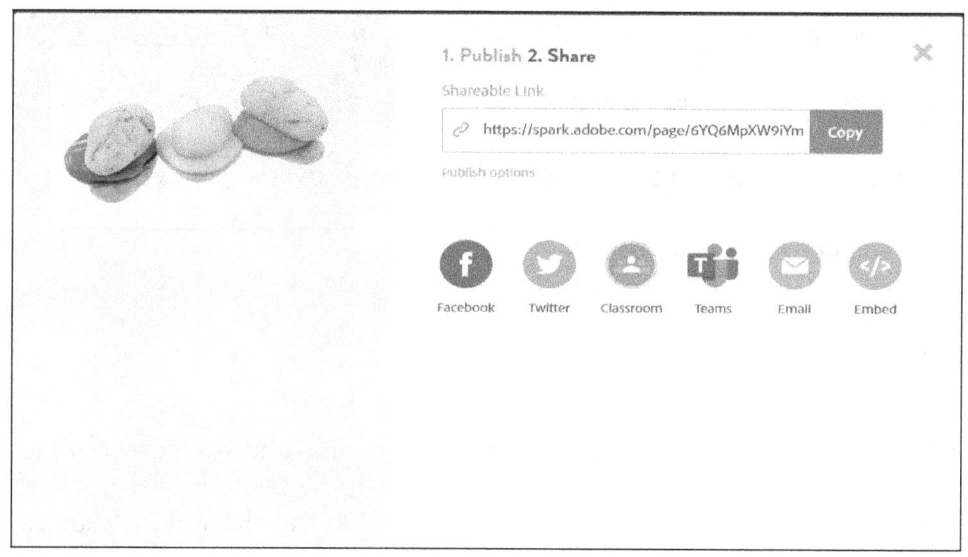

FIGURE 18: Spark Page creating link for sharing

RESULTS AND FINDINGS

Enhance Graphic Designing

Adobe Spark is a free design mobile and web app that allows the users to create and design striking social graphics, web stories and enthusiastic videos by using the tools and the features available. It also enables the users to design their own logo and apply in their projects to make them personalised with few easy tabs. It is exciting and entertaining, as well as quick and easy way to create impressive graphics for any occasion. Adobe Spark helps in escalating the skill to create and edit design. This app provides the users to do any design project that come up using the mobile phone. It enhances the user's facility of creating graphic designs for any occasions by using mobile phones and also enable the users to design graphics incredibly in less stressful process.

A Design Tool for Non-Designers

One of the best advantages of this app is that anyone can create animated videos, web stories and without any knowledge of designing. This design tool is a great help for the non-designers to design fast and in a well organised manner. It is a tool which boost the ability or capacity to do something or act in a particular way in which no expertise is required. It facilitates the user to create web pages and add text, videos, pictures, icons and logo to them. Similarly, users can develop videos having text, pictures, voiceovers, can even add musics to the videos to make an enliven masterwork.

CONCLUSION

In this present framework of imparting education, multimedia plays a pre dominant role. Multimedia has proved to be beneficial in all fields, especially in the field of education by overcoming the obstacles which were very hard to defeat earlier. Now it is considered as one of the key source which can be used at any time and any where for imparting knowledge in multi disciplinary areas. Adobe Spark is considered to be one of the emerging multimedia software with various free features which proves to be effective and excellent mechanism for educational purpose. This tool proves to be very beneficial for the educators by assisting them to gain educational effectiveness. However, measures need to be taken to improvise some of the features of this wonderful software application to make it most appropriate multimedia application for imparting education.

REFERENCES

1. Nagasubramani, P. C., & Raja, R. May 2018. Impact of modern technology in education
2. Sharma, Ppuneet. February 2018. The effectiveness of e-learning for imparting quality education to students
3. Jerem, Bird. Mar 5, 2018. Building truly cross-functional teams
4. Avrith, Tanya. March 31, 2020. Distance Learning with Adobe Spark
5. Bednarz, Jenni. June 30, 2016. Design at a Glance: The Pros and Cons of Canva and Adobe Spark
6. Ahamad, Mohd. Vasim & Abbas, Syed Hauider.Use of Multimedia in Educational Setting
7. Fen, Tan Ai.16th Oct 2017.Multimedia Applications for Educational Purposes
8. https://support.tlt.utah.edu/hc/en-us/articles/360011965711-About-Adobe-Spark

9. htttps://www.ukessays.com/essays/media/multimedia-applications-educational-4151.php

10. https://edtechdigest.com/2019/08/22/adobe-spark-for-education/

11. https://adobespark.zendesk.com/hc/en-us/articles/218922747-What-is-Adobe-Spark-

12. https://spark.adobe.com/features/

13. https://newsghana24.com/why-adobe-spark-suite-is-the-best-for-creators-like-you/

14.   https://ditchthattextbook.com/13-ways-to-create-unforgettable-multimedia-with-adobe-spark/ .Wednesday,October7,2020

SILLY MISTAKES IN REGRESSION ANALYSIS

Prof. Alugolu Avinash
Centurion University of Technology and Management
Andhra Pradesh

INTRODUCTION

Linear regression is a very simple and easy method but has proven to be very advantageous for a large number of time-series data. You can understand how linear regression generally works in a step-by-step process. It is a statistical method that is mostly used for predictive analysis. Linear Regression makes predictions for continuous/real or numeric variables such as sales, salary, age, product price, etc.

The linear regression algorithm shows a linear relationship between a dependent (y) and one or more independent (x) variables, hence called linear regression.

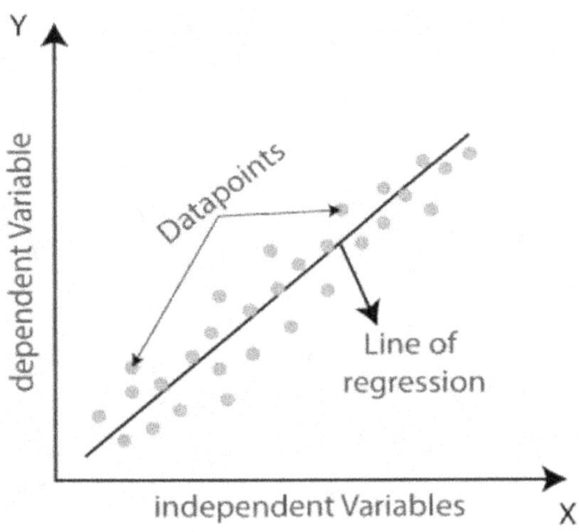

FIGURE 1: Dependent and Independent Variables, Data Points, and Regression Line

MISTAKES IN REGRESSION ANALYSIS

In this study, I have discussed how to avoid simple mistakes while doing Simple Linear Regression.

Mistake 1: Position of the error term in sample and population in the regression equations and also, have you ever checked 'X hat' in any equations of the regression?

The author explains the mistakes that students or programmers or developers do in the structure of the regression equations. So we have some equations on the population side and some equations on the sample side. Let's first talk about the equations that we have on the population side. So over here, I am going to write the regression equations that we have on the population side.

So, the first equation is the expected value of Y given X equal to beta one plus beta two X. The second equation is Y_i is equal to the expected value of Y given X_i plus U_i and the third equation is Y_i equal to beta one plus beta two X_i plus U_i.

$$\text{Expected}(Y/\text{Given } X) = \beta1 + \beta2\ X$$

$$Yi = \text{Expected}(Y/\text{Given } Xi) + Ui$$

$$Yi = \beta1 + \beta2\ Xi + Ui$$

So, these are the three equations that we have on the population side. Note that this first equation is the equation of the population regression line, which you can also call the population regression function. When we write the equation of the population regression line, there is no error in this equation. So, the first equation that I have over here, there is no error term. The error term comes into equation number two and equation number three. The first equation is written on an average level. So, it does not have an edit on the second and the third equation that we have over here. These equations are written at an entity level. So, if you have collected data on different households, then your entities will be households. The left-hand side means the value of the Y variable for the ith household and this Ui means the error of the ith household in the population. The second equation is written at an entity level and when you write the equation at an entity level, then you have to add the error term, so in the first equation, you don't have to add the error term. Many students do this mistake that they write plus Ui over here. So, the first equation you do not have to write, plus Ui but in the second equation, you do have to write plus Ui. Similarly, this third equation that you see over here, this is a combination of equation number one and equation number two. So, from equation number one, you got this relationship. And if you put this relationship over here, then you get this equation number three now, because equation number three is also at an entity level. That means equation number three. Also, you have to write the population error term. So, in this equation, which is the equation of the population regression line, do not add the total and the second and the third equation. You do have to add the error term. These are the three equations that we have on the population side. Let's talk about the three equations that we have on the sample side. Now, see, on the sample side, the counterpart of this equation is Yi (read as Yi hat) equal is β1 (Read β1 hat) plus β2 (Read β2 hat), Xi. The counterpart of the above three equations are

$$Y_i\hat{} = \beta1\hat{} + \beta2\hat{}\, Xi$$

$$Y_i = Y_i\hat{} + Ui\hat{}$$

$$Y_i = \beta1\hat{} + \beta2\hat{}\, Xi + Ui\hat{}$$

These are the three equations that we have on the sample side. Now see, even on the sample side, you have to pay attention to this equation first. This is the equation of the sample regression line. You can also call it a sample decryption function. When you write the equation of the sample regression line, you do not add the error term. So, there is no error term in this first equation that you have over here. If you take a look at the second and the third equation, you do have an error term in the second and the third equation. The error term will only come into the picture when on the left-hand side you have Yi in the first equation does have an error term. This is one of the mistakes that I have seen many students making. They do not understand in which equations they have to put the editor. So, I hope you have got some clarity from here that in the first equation, that is this equation and this equation does not put the error term. And in the second and the third equation, you have to put the editor the notation that I am using for the population error term is Ui.

Mistake 2: Identifying the difference between the summation of Ui^ square and the summation of Ui^ whole square

In this section, I want the learners to pay attention to the difference between the summation of Ui^ square and the summation of Ui^ whole square.

$$\sum Ui^{\wedge 2}$$

$$\left(\sum Ui^{\wedge}\right)^2$$

So, basically when we work for the method of OLS, we choose $\beta 1^{\wedge}$, $\beta 2^{\wedge}$ such that summation of $\sum Ui^{\wedge 2}$ is minimized. First of all, $Ui^{\wedge}$ is the notation that I'm using for the sample. We have one more name for this which is residuals.

Mistake 3: Not checking the mathematical expressions for the model.

$$\sum(Xi - X') (Yi-Y') = \sum (Xi-X')(Yi)$$

$$\sum(Xi - X') (Yi-Y') = \sum(Yi-Y') (Xi-X')$$

$$\sum(Y_i-Y') (X_i - X') = \sum(Y_i-Y') (X_i)$$

Many students tried to use this shortcut, again and again. I have seen students walking with this expression and then writing this expression as $\sum X_i Y_i$ by saying that we can remove X'. Well, you cannot. Do not remove X' or Y' in any expression, which leads to wrong results. So be careful with these mathematical expressions as well.

Mistake 4: Sample error considerations

I am going to discuss the population error which is Ui and the sample error Ui^. Note one thing over here that sees the population error is something that you do not know. So, this is unknown because we do not have the population data. But Ui^ is something which is known. value reading, simple in integration, you will see that. Well, this is one of the wrong things. You would never put assumptions on the sample. I mean, think of it in this manner, that sampling error is something that you already know. So, for example, you are going to collect the sample data. Once you collect the sample data, you will use that sample data to find the values of β1^, β2 ^. Which are your estimates? Once you have the values of β1^, β2 ^ you can use those values to find the values of Ui^. So, once you have the sample data, you will get to know the values of the sample errors. And if you have the values of the sample errors, why we have to put any assumptions on the sample. We put assumptions on the population error because population error is something that we do not have data on. So, we put some assumptions on the mean of the population error. We also put some assumptions on the variance of the population error. We never put any assumptions on the mean of the sampling error. Neither we put any assumptions on the variance of the sampling error. Because sample error is something that we already know. So. there is no need to assume anything about that. If you want to find anything related to the sample, do you have the data? You can just use that data to find it. This is also one of the things that you should keep in mind, that whatever assumptions you are going to encounter, the assumptions are going to be related to the population error. We do not put assumptions on the sampling error. The next thing that you should keep in mind is the mathematical expression for $Ui^{\wedge}$. Which is the sampling error? Students do remember that $Ui^{\wedge}$ is the difference between the actual Y values. So, there are some actual values. By actual, by values. I mean the values that you have collected. Divide values that are part of the data that you have collected. And there is something called fritted by values. These are the two types of values that we have. The notation that we have for the actual by values is Y_i. And in addition to that, we have for the frigid by values as $Y_i{}^{\wedge}$. Now, many of the students do remember the part, what is the difference between the actual Y values, and defeated Y values. They just do not remember the detection of the difference. That means they do not remember whether we have to do by minus, $Y^{\wedge}$ or we have done the other way around. That is $Y^{\wedge} - Y_i$. You need to keep this thing in your mind that $Y^{\wedge}$, which is your sample error, is equal to the actual value minus the defeated value and not the other way around. So, this is also one of the mistakes that I have seen many students making.

Mistake 5: Not concentrating on the assumptions and Connectivities

In this section, I am going to discuss the assumptions of the classical linear regression model that you encounter by studying simple linear regression. One of the mistakes that students do by studying simple linear regression is that they do not pay enough attention to these assumptions. See, you have to understand this, but the assumptions that you see in simple linear regression are quite important, and you will see these assumptions again and again. For example, whatever assumption you are going to read in simple linear regression you will have an extension of these assumptions in multiple linear regression at a later stage. You will also see that there will be some contexts where we will violate these assumptions one by one, and then we will see how the framework is going to change. So, if you do not have a good understanding of the assumptions while you are doing simple linear regression you are going to struggle in connecting with the dots. Whenever you are reading these assumptions, make sure that you spend a good amount of time understanding these. The beauty of simple linear regression is that you are only working with two variables and when you look at two variables you can also make scatter plots and try to visualize these assumptions which will also help you with the understanding.

Mistake 6: Standard Errors or Standard Deviation?

This section discusses the difference between standard deviation and standard error. So, you must have seen this formula of the variance of $\beta_2\hat{}$.

$$\text{Variance } (\beta_2\hat{}) = \sigma^2 / \sum(Xi - X')^2$$

Simple Linear Regression $Y_i = \beta1\hat{} + \beta2\hat{}\ Xi + Ui\hat{}$ where $Ui\hat{}$ is sample error and $\beta1\hat{}$, $\beta2\hat{}$ are the estimators. This is the formula that we have four variants of beta two hat. Now see if you take under the root of this formula then it is called the standard deviation of $\beta2\hat{}$.

$$\text{Standard Deviation} = \sqrt{(\text{Variance } (\beta_2\hat{}))} = \sqrt{(\sigma^2 / \sum(Xi - X')^2)}$$

This is how you define the standard deviation of beta to hot, but we never work with standard deviation. Sigma squared, and if you remember the assumption of almost getting us to the Sigma Square that you see over here, this is the variance of the population error. If you do not have any data on the population error, that means you cannot find the value of the variance of the population error. This Sigma Square that you see over here, this is unknown. What we do is that we replace the Sigma Square over here with Sigma hat squared. So this is a replacement. That we have and sigma hat squared is defined as the summation of $Ui\hat{}$ squared divided by n-2.

$$\sigma^2 = \sum Ui^2 / n\text{-}2$$

Where $\sum Ui^2$ is called residuals sum of squares what is it that we are going to do all the time?

We will always replace sigma squared with sigma hat squared. As soon as you do this replacement, you do not get an actual variance of $\beta_2^{\wedge}$ now, you get an estimated variance of $\beta_2^{\wedge}$. And when you take the root of estimated variance of $\beta_2^{\wedge}$ that you had the term that we have for that is called the standard error of beta two hat and not standard deviation. Look at the difference between the standard deviation and Standard Errors in the above equations. The standard deviation has sigma square and actual variance also has sigma square. The standard error has sigma hat squared and the estimated variance also has sigma hat squared.

UNIVARIATE LINEAR REGRESSION

Step 1: Download the dataset and importing libraries

```
In [77]:  import numpy as nu
          import pandas as pa
          import seaborn as se
          import matplotlib.pyplot as pl
          from sklearn import preprocessing, svm
          from sklearn.model_selection import train_test_split
          from sklearn.linear_model import LinearRegression
```

FIGURE 2: Importing necessary libraries

Step 2: Reading the dataset

It is considered that the two variables are linearly associated. So, we try to identify a linear function that makes prediction the response value(y) as perfectly as possible as a method of the feature or independent variable(x).

Let us assume a sample dataset where we have a value of outcome y for every input value x:

Table 1: Sample data points for linear regression

x	0	1	2	3	4	5	6	7	8	9
y	1	3	2	5	7	8	8	9	10	12

For overview, we state like:

x as **input vector**, i.e $x = [x1, x2, ..., xn]$

y as **output vector**, i.e $y = [y1, y2, ..., yn]$

for **N** data points (in above sample data, N=10).

A scatter plot of the above data points is presented in Figure 3:

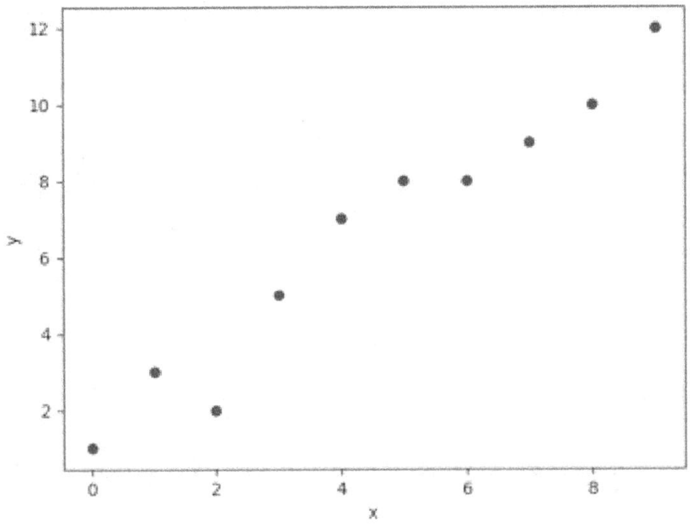

FIGURE 3: Scatter plot for given data points.

Now, the work is to identify a line that fits best in the mentioned scatter plot so that we can

do the prediction of the response for any new input values. (i.e an input of x not available in the dataset or data points). This line is identified as the regression line. The equation of the regression line looks as:

$$A(X_i) = B_0 + B_1 X_i$$

Here A(Xi) indicates the prediction value for i^{th} observation, B_0 and B_1 are regression coefficients and indicates y-axis intercept and slope value of regression line correspondingly. Implementation of the linear regression model using Python and Sklearn is given below.

PYTHON PROGRAM

```
*I.py - C:/Users/lenovo/AppData/Local/Programs/Python/Python38-32/I.py (3.8.5)*
File  Edit  Format  Run  Options  Window  Help
import numpy as np
import pandas as pd
from sklearn.model_selection import train_test_split

data = pd.read_csv("Book1.csv")
print("data points are\n",data)
x = data['x']
x = np.array(x)
x = x.reshape(-1,1)
print("x data is\n",x)
y = data['y']
y = np.array(y)
y = y.reshape(-1,1)
print("y data is",y)
X_train,X_test,y_train, y_test = train_test_split(x,y,test_size=0.2,random_state=1)
from sklearn.linear_model import LinearRegression
object1 = LinearRegression()
object1.fit(X_train,y_train)
print("coef value is\n",object1.coef_)
print("intecept value is\n",object1.intercept_)
y_pred = object1.predict(X_test)

from sklearn import metrics
print("MAE is\n",metrics.mean_absolute_error(y_test,y_pred))
print("MSE is \n5",metrics.mean_squared_error(y_test,y_pred))
print("Accuracy is",metrics.r2_score(y_test,y_pred))
```

FIGURE 4: Python implementation of linear regression using Sklearn module

OUTPUT

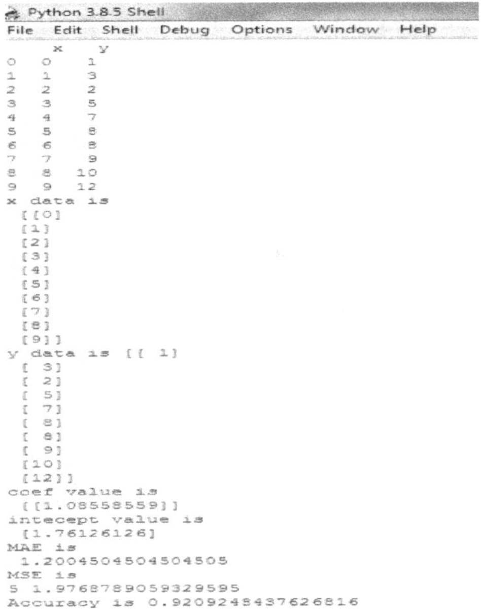

FIGURE 5: Output of Linear Regression using Sklearn module

It is observed that with the test size 20% we have received an accuracy value of 92 %.

CONCLUSION

Regression study is used in the wider sense; but, firstly it depends on quantifying the alternates in the dependent variable (regressed variable) required to the changes in the independent variable with the data on the dependent variables. This is due to all the regression models whether non-linear or linear simple or multiples relate to the dependent variable with the independent variables.

REFERENCES

1. S. Ray, "A Quick Review of Machine Learning Algorithms," 2019 International Conference on Machine Learning, Big Data, Cloud and Parallel Computing (COMITCon), Faridabad, India, 2019, pp. 35-39, DOI: 10.1109/COMITCon.2019.8862451.

2. H. Hirose, Y. Soejima and K. Hirose, "NNRMLR: A Combined Method of Nearest Neighbor Regression and Multiple Linear Regression," 2012 IIAI International Conference on Advanced Applied Informatics, Fukuoka, 2012, pp. 351-356, DOI: 10.1109/IIAI-AAI.2012.76.

3. Z. Cao, L. Liu, and O. Markowitch, "Comment on "Highly Efficient Linear Regression Outsourcing to a Cloud"," in IEEE Transactions on Cloud Computing, vol. 7, no. 3, pp. 893-893, 1 July-Sept. 2019, DOI: 10.1109/TCC.2017.2709299.

4. D. Wang, Y. Gao and Z. Tian, "One-Variable Linear Regression Mathematical Model of Color Reading and Material Concentration Identification," 2017 International Conference on Smart City and Systems Engineering (ICSCSE), Changsha, 2017, pp. 119-122, DOI: 10.1109/ICSCSE.2017.37.

5. N. S. Patil and M. F. Yaligar, "Analysis of linear relation between P-value and co relational value using R programming," 2017 International Conference on Advances in Computing, Communications and Informatics (ICACCI), Udupi, 2017, pp. 983-987, DOI: 10.1109/ICACCI.2017.8125969.

6. B. Sravani and M. M. Bala, "Prediction of Student Performance Using Linear Regression," 2020 International Conference for Emerging Technology (INCET), Belgaum, India, 2020, pp. 1-5, doi: 10.1109/INCET49848.2020.9154067.

7. R. K. Grace and B. Suganya, "Machine Learning based Rainfall Prediction," 2020 6th International Conference on Advanced Computing and Communication Systems (ICACCS), Coimbatore, India, 2020, pp. 227-229, doi: 10.1109/ICACCS48705.2020.9074233.

8. S. G. Iyer and A. D. Pawar, "Machine Learning Model for Predicting Price of Processors using Multivariate Linear Regression," 2019 International Conference on Smart Systems and Inventive Technology (ICSSIT), Tirunelveli, India, 2019, pp. 52-56, doi: 10.1109/ICSSIT46314.2019.8987936.

OBJECT DETECTION AND ANALYSIS USING AMAZON REKOGNITION

Prof. Raj Kumar Mohanta
Assistant Professor
Centurion University of Technology and Management
Odisha, India

INTRODUCTION

Image processing is a method to perform some operations on an image, in order to get an enhanced image or to extract some useful information from it. It is a type of signal processing in which the input is an image and the output may be image or characteristics/features associated with that image. The purpose of image processing is to improve the quality of the image by removing the disturbances. It consists of various techniques such as Image segmentation, enhancement, classification, restoration, pattern recognition, extraction etc. So our objective is to study how AWS Rekognition can be used for object detection along with Facial Analysis, Image Moderation, Face Comparison, Celebrity Recognition, Text in Image and Video Analysis.

WHAT IS A PATTERN?

A pattern is an arrangement of descriptors or features. It could be a human face, any image, speech signal, finger print, a hand written etc. A pattern class is a family of patterns that share common properties. Pattern classes are denoted w_1, w_2, w_3..., w_n where n is the number of classes. A pattern is a series of data that repeats in a recognizable way. It can be identified in the history of the asset being evaluated or other assets with similar characteristics.

INTRODUCTION TO PATTERN RECOGNITION

Pattern recognition is the study of how machines can observe the environment, learn to distinguish patterns of interest from their background, and make sound and reasonable decisions about the categories of the patterns. Pattern recognition by machine involves techniques for assigning pattern to their respective classes-automatically and with as little human intervention as possible. For recognizing an object the system must receive some information or features from that object. Based on these features the object is assigned with one of the possible classes. Pattern recognition means identification of ideal object. In practice three common pattern arrangements used which are vectors (for quantitative descriptions), strings and trees (for structural descriptions). Recognition technique based on matching represent each class by a prototype pattern vector. An unknown pattern is assigned to the class to which it is closet in terms of a predefined metrics. The simplest approach is the minimum distance classifier which computes the distance between the unknown and each of the prototype vectors. It chooses the smallest distance to make a decision. The statistical properties of the pattern classes in a problem often are unknown or cannot be estimated. In practice, such decision theoretic problems are best handled by methods that yield the required decision functions directly through training. The measuring and interpreting physical events, probability consideration become important in pattern recognition because of the randomness under which pattern classes normally are generated. It is possible to derive a classification approach that is optimal in the sense that, on average its use yields the lowest probability of committing classification errors. The design of a pattern recognition system essentially involves the following three aspects:

- Data acquisition and preprocessing

- Data representation

- Decision making

The problem domain dictates the choice of sensor(s), preprocessing technique, representation scheme, and the decision making model. It is generally agreed that a well-defined and sufficiently constrained recognition problem (small intra-class variations and large interclass variations) will lead to a compact pattern representation and a simple decision making strategy. Learning from a set of examples (training set) is an important and desired attribute of most pattern recognition systems.

The four best known approaches for pattern recognition are:

1. Template matching

2. Statistical classification

3. Syntactic or structural matching

4. Artificial Neural networks.

Pattern recognition is generally categorized according to the type of learning procedure used to generate the output value. Supervised learning assumes that a set of training data (the training set) has been provided, consisting of a set of instances that have been properly labeled by hand with the correct output. A learning procedure then generates a model that attempts to meet two sometimes conflicting objectives: Perform as well as possible on the training data, and generalize as well as possible to new data. An Unsupervised learning, on the other hand, assumes training data that has not been hand-labeled, and attempts to find inherent patterns in the data that can then be used to determine the correct output value for new data instances. A combination of the two that has recently been explored is semi-supervised learning, which uses a combination of labeled and unlabeled data (typically a small set of labeled data combined with a large amount of unlabeled data).

1. What is Object Detection?

Object detection is a computer technology related to computer vision and image processing that deals with detecting instances of semantic objects of a certain class (such as humans, buildings, or cars) in digital images and videos. Well-researched domains of object detection include face detection and pedestrian detection. Object detection has applications in many areas of computer vision, including image retrieval and video surveillance. Methods for object detection generally fall into either machine learning-based approaches or deep learning-based approaches. For Machine Learning approaches, it becomes necessary to first define features using one of the methods below, then using a technique such as support vector machine (SVM) to do the classification. On the other hand, deep learning techniques are able to do end-to-end object detection without specifically defining features, and are typically based on convolutional neural networks (CNN).

Object detection and object recognition are similar techniques for identifying objects, but they vary in their execution. Object detection is the process of finding instances of objects in images. In the case of deep learning, object detection is a subset of object recognition, where the object is not only identified but also located in an image. This allows for multiple objects to be identified and located within the same image.

2. Review of Literature

For the past few years a lots of studies had been carried out on pattern recognition. In [4], authors proposed interactive voice response (IVR) with pattern recognition based on neural networks. In this case after entering the correct password the user is asked to input his voice sample which can be used to verify his voice. The addition of voice pattern recognition in the authentication process enhances the security. The results are promising based on false accept and false reject criteria having a quick response time. Here a Multilayer perceptron is used for feature matching. Authors in [5] used artificial neural network for face recognition. They evaluated the performance of the system by applying two photometric normalization techniques: Histogram equalization and Homomorphic filtering. The system produced promising results for face verification and face recognition.

In [6], the authors used artificial neural network for Electrocardiogram (ECG) pattern recognition. Four types of ECG patterns were chosen from the MIT-BIH database to be recognized, which includes normal sinus rhythms (N), premature ventricular contraction (PVC) and aterial premature beat (A) and left bundle branch block beat (L). Recognizing an ECG pattern is essentially the process of extracting and classifying ECG feature parameters which may be obtained either from the time domain or transform domain. In this method the performance of the neural networks was evaluated by the recognition sensitivities, the overall recognition accuracy and the number of neurons needed. The overall accuracy is defined as the ratio of the total number of beats recognized correctly to the total number of beats in the test phase. In [7] authors applied artificial neural network approach for optical character recognition (OCR). A simple feed forward neural network model has been trained with different set of noisy data. The back-propagation method was used for learning in neural network. The application includes postal code recognition, banking, reading devices for blind etc.

AMAZON REKOGNITION

Amazon Rekognition makes it easy to add image and video analysis to your applications using proven, highly scalable, deep learning technology that requires no machine learning expertise to use. With Amazon Rekognition, you can identify objects, people, text, scenes, and activities in images and videos, as well as detect any inappropriate content. Amazon

Rekognition also provides highly accurate facial analysis and facial search capabilities that you can use to detect, analyze, and compare faces for a wide variety of user verification, people counting, and public safety use cases. Amazon Rekognition provides two API sets. You use Amazon Rekognition Image for analyzing images and Amazon Rekognition Video for analyzing videos. When a customer uploads a photo, your application can use Amazon Rekognition Image to detect real-world objects or faces in the image. With Amazon Rekognition Custom Labels, you can identify the objects and scenes in images that are specific to your business needs. For example, you can build a model to classify specific machine parts on your assembly line or to detect unhealthy plants. Amazon Rekognition Custom Labels takes care of the heavy lifting of model development for you, so no machine learning experience is required. You simply need to supply images of objects or scenes you want to identify, and the service handles the rest.

A label or a tag is an object, scene, or concept found in an image or video based on its contents. For example, a photo of people on a tropical beach may contain labels such as Person, Water, Sand, Palm Tree, and Swimwear (objects), Beach (scene) and Outdoors (concept). Amazon Rekognition Video can also detect activities such as a person skiing or riding a bike. Amazon Rekognition Image does not detect activities in images. Amazon Rekognition Image and Amazon Rekognition Video can return the bounding box for common object labels such as people, cars, furniture, apparel or pets. Bounding box information isn't returned for less common object labels. You can use bounding boxes to find the exact locations of objects in an image, count instances of detected objects, or to measure an object's size using bounding box dimensions.

Key features

- **Labels**

With Amazon Rekognition, you can identify thousands of objects (such as bike, telephone, building), and scenes (such as parking lot, beach, city). When analyzing video, you can also identify specific activities such as "delivering a package" or "playing soccer".

FIGURE 1 Example of Labels

- **Content Moderation**

Amazon Rekognition helps you identify potentially unsafe or inappropriate content across both image and video assets and provides you with detailed labels that allow you to accurately control what you want to allow based on your needs.

FIGURE 2 Example of Content Moderation

- **Face Detection and Analysis**

With Amazon Rekognition, you can easily detect when faces appear in images and videos and get attributes such as gender, age range, eyes open, glasses, facial hair for each. In video, you can also measure how these faces attributes change over time, such as constructing a timeline of the emotions expressed by an actor.

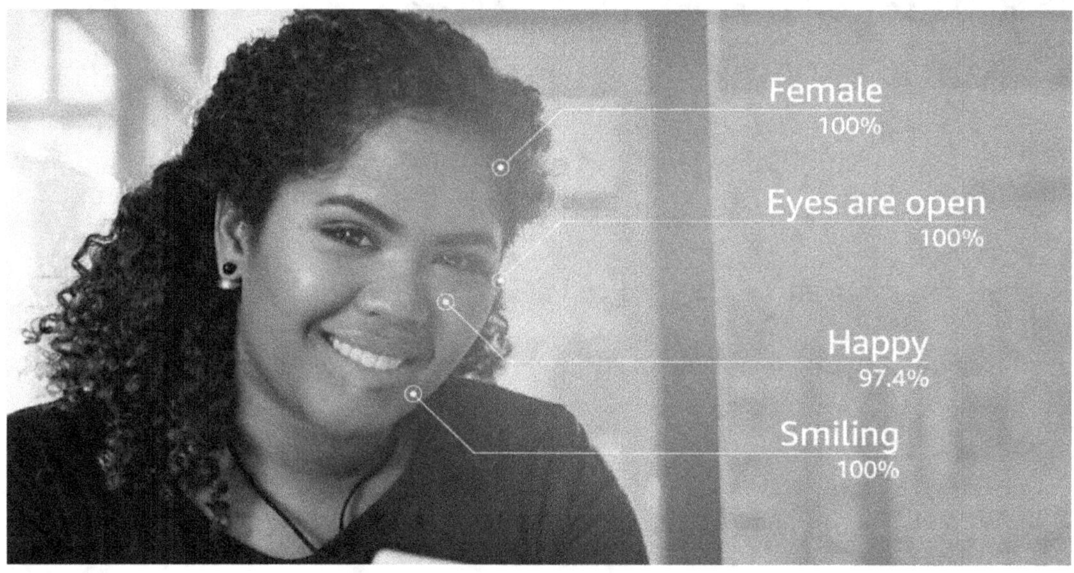

FIGURE 3 Example of Face Detection and Analysis

- **Custom Labels**

With Amazon Rekognition Custom Labels, you can extend the detection capabilities of Amazon Rekognition to extract information from images that is uniquely helpful to your business. For example, you can find your corporate logo in social media, identify your products on store shelves, classify your machine parts in an assembly line, or detect your animated characters in videos.

FIGURE 4 Example of Custom Labels

- **Text Detection**

In photos and videos, text appears very differently than neat words on a printed page. Amazon Rekognition can read skewed and distorted text to capture information like store names, forced narratives overlaid on media, street signs, and text on product packaging.

FIGURE 5 Example of Text Detection

- **Face Search and Verification**

Amazon Rekognition provides fast an accurate face search, allowing you to identify a person in a photo or video using your private repository of face images. You can also verify identity by analyzing a face image against images you have stored for comparison.

FIGURE 6 Example of Face Search and Verification

- **Celebrity Recognition**

Amazon Rekognition can recognize thousands of celebrities in a wide range of categories, such as entertainment and media, sports, business, and politics. With Amazon Rekognition, you can recognize celebrities in images and in stored videos. You can also get additional information for recognized celebrities. The Amazon Rekognition celebrity recognition API is tuned to detect celebrities in different settings, cosmetic makeup, and other conditions. Social, media, and entertainment customers can build apps that use celebrity recognition. Amazon Rekognition celebrity recognition is designed to be exclusively used in cases where you expect there may be a known celebrity in an image or a video.

FIGURE 7 Example of Celebrity Recognition

Output

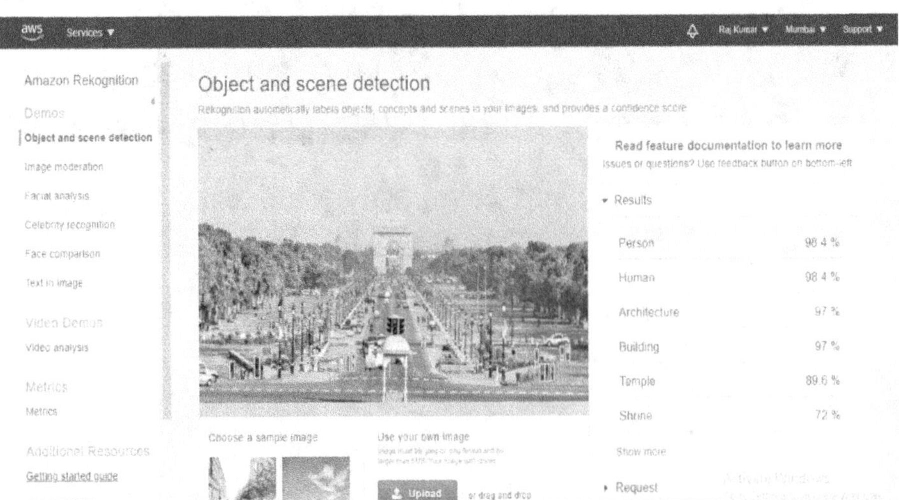

FIGURE 8 Object and Scene detection using Amazon Rekognition

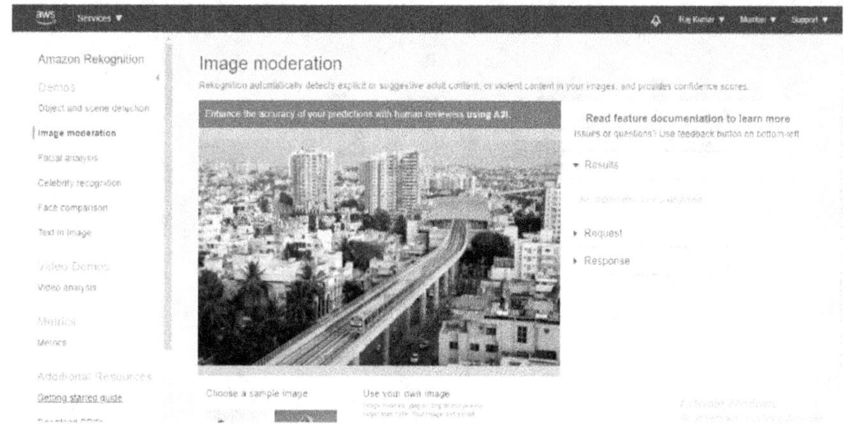

FIGURE 9 Image Moderation using Amazon Rekognition

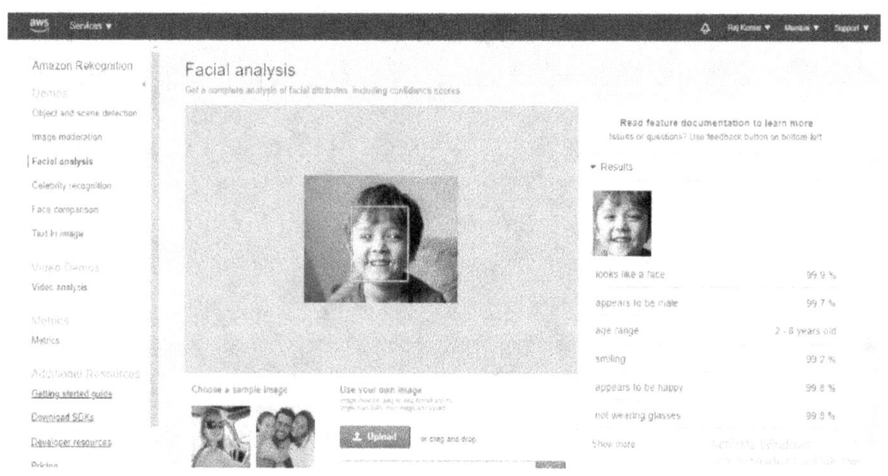

FIGURE 10 Facial Analysis using Amazon Rekognition

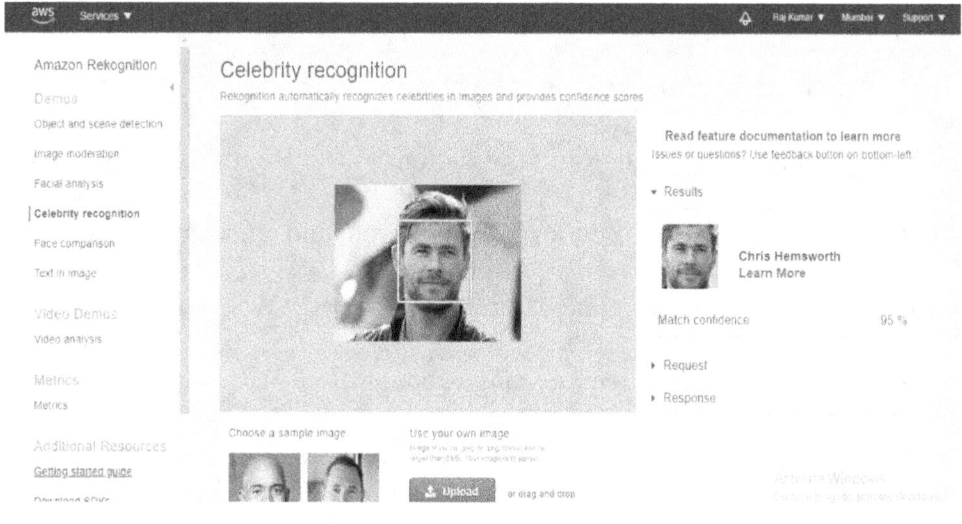

FIGURE 11 Celebrity recognition using Amazon Rekognition

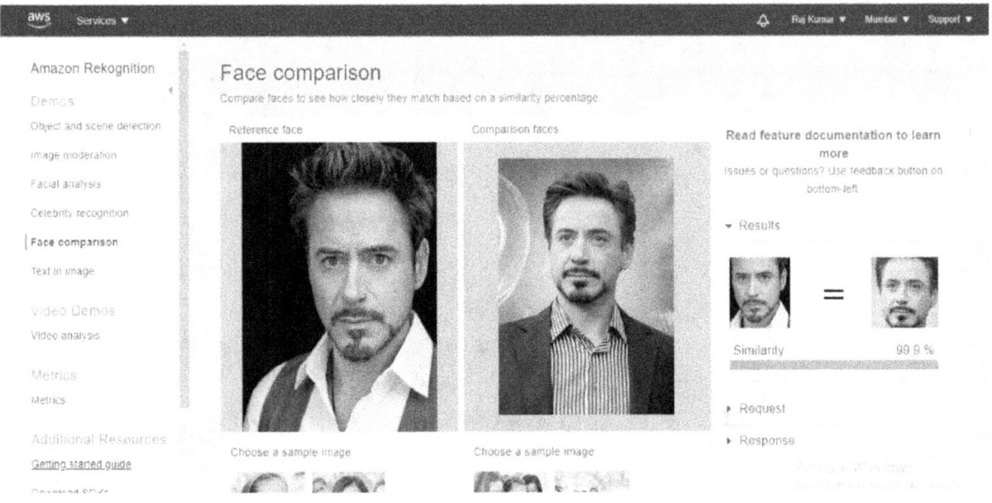

FIGURE 12 Face Comparison using Amazon Rekognition

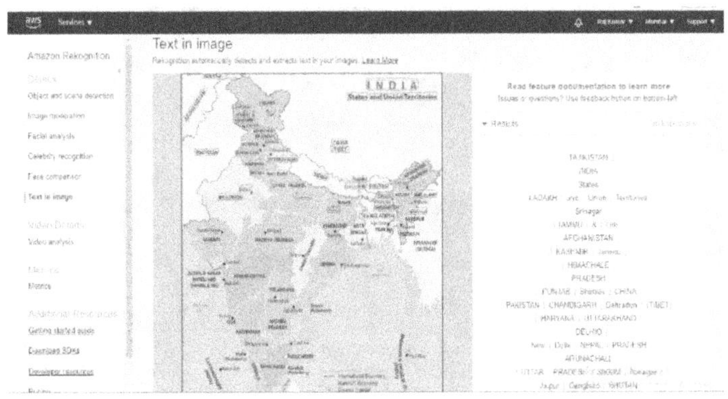

FIGURE 13 Text in Image using Amazon Rekognition

CONCLUSION

Amazon Rekognition is a service that makes it easy and quick to add deep learning-based visual search and image classification to your applications. With Rekognition, you can detect objects, scenes and faces in images. You can also search and compare faces, recognize celebrities, and identify inappropriate content. Integrated with AWS, Amazon Rekognition provides a fast, scalable, reliable and secure image recognition platform to help customers cost effectively gain fast insight and new revenue opportunities from their image library at the scale of their business. Rekognition also provides highly accurate facial analysis and facial search capabilities that you can use to detect, analyze, and compare faces for a wide variety of user verification, people counting, and public safety use cases.

REFERENCES

[1]   Raj Kumar Mohanta, Binapani Sethi, "A Study on Application of Artificial Neural Network and Genetic Algorithm in Pattern Recognition", IJCSET, Vol.3 No.2 February 2012.

[2]   https://aws.amazon.com/rekognition/

[3]   https://ap-south1.console.aws.amazon.com/rekognition/home?region=ap-south-1#/

[4]   Syed Ayaz Ali Shah, Azzam ul Asar and S.F.Shaukat, "Neural Network Solution for Secure Interactive Voice Response", World Applied Sciences Journal 6 (9), 1264-1269, 2009.

[5]   Raj Kumar Mohanta, Binapani Sethi, "Amazon Recognition in Pattern Recognition", JES, Vol.11 No.6 June 2020.

[6]   Shahrin Azuan Nazeer, Nazaruddin Omar, Khairol Faisal Jumari and Marzuki Khalid, "Face detecting using Artificial Neural Networks Approach", First Asia International Conference on Modelling & Simulation, 2007.

[7]   Lin He, Wensheng Hou, Xiaolin Zhen and Chenglin Peng, "Recognition of ECG Patterns Using Artificial Neural Network", Sixth International Conference on Intelligent Systems Design and Applications, Volume 02, 2006,.

[8]   Nallasamy Mani and Bala Srinivasan, "Application of Artificial Neural Network Model for Optical Character Recognition", IEEE international conference, 12-15 Oct, 1997.

[9]   D.Fogel, "What is evolutionary computing", IEEE spectrum magazine, Feb 2000.

VIRTUALIZATION FRAMEWORK FOR BIG DATA APPLICATION

Dr. Debendra Maharana
Centurion University of Technology & Management
Odisha, India

INTRODUCTION

Recently with the rapid growth of emerging applications that lead to the huge growth of data size, which contains variety of data such as structured, semi-structured and unstructured have resulted in a newer way of processing these big data using virtualization framework in order to get meaningful insights and improve performance. Virtualization combined with big data is an emerging technique which has been used extensively in research for a long time. The main purpose of this paper is to familiarize and find out the relationship between Big Data and Virtualization. The main focus has been given to some of the applications of Big Data that use Virtualization framework in different fields in all diverse aspects . In this chapter, current state-of-the-art of virtualization approaches and technologies in the context of Big Data have been analysed which can guide to better design and deploy big data applications for improving the system performance .

Three characteristics of virtualization that support the scalability and operating efficiency required for big data environments are(Zaineb t. Al-azez 2019):

- **Partitioning**: In virtualization the available resources is partitioned to support many applications and operating systems in a single physical system.

- **Isolation:** Since each virtual machine is isolated from its host physical system , the host system and the other virtual machines are not affected even if one virtual instance crashes.

- **Encapsulation:** A virtual machine can be identified easily as it is represented as a single file based on the services it provides.

In this chapter an overview of the current state of virtualization approaches and technologies in the context of Big Data tasks solution is provided. The rest of the chapter is organized as , in section 2 the basics of virtualization technologies is analysed, together with the brief overview of most popular open-source virtualization solutions. Section 3 is devoted to the main results on the comparison of containerization and virtualization solutions .In the last Section, the conclusions on the performed analysis and future scope is provided.

VIRTUALIZATION FRAMEWORK

Virtualization was developed for abstracting the hardware and system resources to provide simultaneous execution of several operating systems on a single hardware platform (Zaineb t. Al-azez 2019). Virtualization technologies based on Hypervisor and container come with different trade-offs and each want to achieve different goals. Both types of virtualization make it easy to migrate and allow a better resource utilization because of hardware abstraction, leading to lower costs and saving energy. The two different virtualization frameworks is studied in this section,, i.e., Docker container and virtual machine (VM) hypervisor which is also called Virtual Machine Monitor (VMM). Application can directly run on each VM by calling appropriate library as each VM has its own OS.

There are three different techniques used for virtualization (Chris Horne 2007)

1. **Full Virtualization.** In this approach, user mode code runs directly on CPU without any translation.
2. **Hardware Assisted Full Virtualization**. To support virtualization and to make virtualization simpler ,new features have been developed by the hardware vendor.

Privileged and sensitive calls are set to automatically trap to the VMM, removing the need for either binary translation or para-virtualization.

3. **Par-avirtualization**. This technique requires modification of the guest kernel. The non-virtualizable/privileged instructions in the source code of the guest kernel are replaced with hypercalls which directly call the hypervisor. The hypervisor provides hypercall interfaces for kernel operations like memory management, interrupt handling, and communication to devices. It differs from full virtualization, where unmodified guest kernel is used and the guest OS does not know that it is running in a virtualized environment(Chris Horne 2007).

HYPERVISOR-BASED VIRTUALIZATION

The basic principle of hypervisor based virtualization is to emulate the underlying physical hardware and create virtual hardware(Figure 1), and an operating system is installed on the top of these newly created virtual hardware. The hypervisor has the control of all the hardware resources and can take away resources from one VM to give it to another. The hypervisor also maintains the state of all the VMs at all the times. It does these by trapping all the privileged instructions executed by the guest VM and emulating the resource they access. The hypervisor is responsible for emulating all the hardware devices and providing proper resource isolation between multiple machines running on the same physical machine to yield better system efficiency.

It abstracts the computer hardware, system resources (CPU, memory, network, storage) and think as a single machine to go even it has many Virtual machines. Each Host machine can run multiple VMs with the Hypervisor based middleware software

(VMM). Each Virtual Machine consists of Guest OS in addition to the Libraries necessary for the applications.

Hypervisor-based virtualization allows the virtual machine and its applications to directly access the CPU in an unprivileged mode (Janki Bhimani 2017), resulting in performance improvements.

In the industry in Hypervisor-based virtualization two different types of Virtualization are are used, one is Hosted virtualization(Type-1) and the other is Bare Metal Virtualization(Type-2). A Bare-metal hypervisor runs directly on the physical hardware while the hosted hypervisor runs on top of conventional operating systems. Examples includes VMware Workstation, Microsoft's Virtual PC.

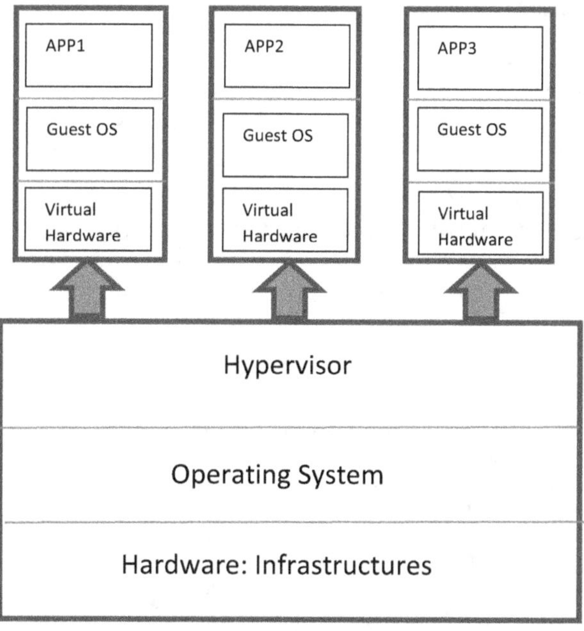

FIGURE 1: Hypervisor-Based Virtualization

CONTAINER-BASED VIRTUALIZATION

The container virtualization is done at the OS level in contrast to hypervisor-based virtualization which is virtualizing hardware resources at the hardware level. Since containers use the hardware of the host system without a virtual hardware emulation, it provides a separated environment, like virtualization where every container run their own operating system by sharing the same single kernel and the software running in containers communicate directly with the host kernel of the system.Each container has their own file system , network stack etc. Docker, LXC ,etc are the examples of Container based virtualization .

Figure 2 depicts the Container-based virtualization shares the single kernel with multiple Containers installed on top of it. Here the host kernel performs resource management for Containers. The advantage of Container-based virtualization is to provide scalability and operational flexibility.

There are two types of Containers.

- Application Container

- System Container

The container which having a single application is called "Application Container", those who maintained the complete operating system along with multiple process and services instead of single Application is called "System Container".

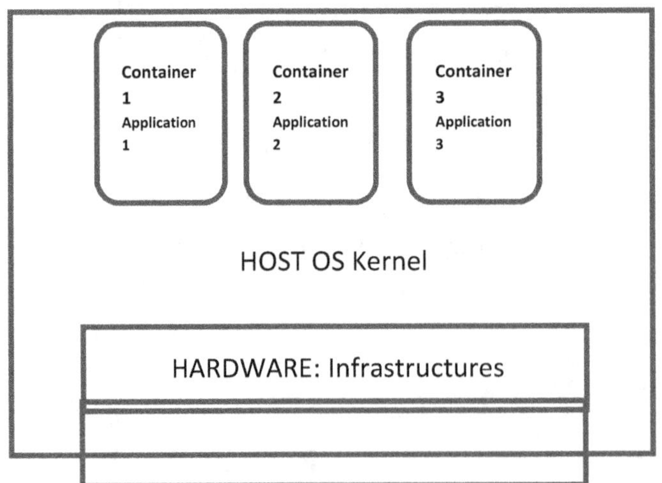

FIGURE 2: Container-Based Virtualization

Though hypervisor-based virtualization technology has been used successfully in many applications to deploy high-performance and scalable infrastructure but now container-based virtualization techniques are becoming an important option for use due to their lightweight operation and better scaling as compared to Virtual Machines (VM). With containerization techniques such as Docker becoming mature and promising better performance and used to speed-up big data applications(Radu F 2016).

1. COMPARISON OF CONTAINERIZATION AND VIRTUALIZATION SOLUTIONS

Containers and virtual machines are two different technologies. Each has its own advantages and working patterns. As each containers are sitting on top of the same kernel, and sharing most of the base operating system, containers are much smaller and light weight compared to a virtualized guest operating system. As they are light weight an operating system can have many containers running on top of it, compared to the limited number of guest operating system that we can run. The Docker containers are lightweight when compared to VMs as each container does not have to operate separate OS (operating system) (Janki Bhimani 2017). Containers perform shared resource management but VMs perform distributed resource management. The distributed resource management in VM guarantees stability and security because each virtual machine runs with its specific assigned set of resources, while shared resource management in Docker enables more flexible sharing of resources to increase overall resource utilization. It is observed that for many different applications, containerization techniques like Docker, LxCs etc. have promising performance.Table I compare performance of widely used Big Data processing framework on Docker with that of traditional virtual machines(Radu F 2016).

TABLE 1: Difference between VM hypervisor and Docker container

Spec	Virtual Machine	Container
Products	VMware, Xen, KVM, etc.	Dockers, rkt, etc.
virtualization Controller	VM hypervisor	Docker engine
Resource Management	Distributed	Shared
Guest OS	Included	Not included
Launch Time	Long	Short

(i)   **Virtualization Controller**: Virtualization controller that runs on the host is required to manage multiple virtualization instances for the termination, instantiation and inspect low-level information like network ports and IP addresses of all instances. VM hypervisor is present as a controller in the virtual machine, while Docker contains Docker engine.

(ii)   **Guest OS**: Since Docker does not maintain a guest OS inside each container, it makes containers "lighter" and in each instance it lowers the overhead of managing device drivers . compared to ,Containers enable faster start up with better performance. Furthermore, containers have less isolation by sharing the host's kernel.

(iii)   **Resource Management**: Since each VM's hypervisor has distributed resource management , so each VM can use the maximum limit of resources. Many smart techniques are exists to distribute resources in an optimal way among different virtual machines, but they lack in run time flexibility. The Docker container relies on cgroups to assign, allocate and manage resources like Memory, Block I/O, Network, CPU etc.

   Unlike VM, containerized virtualization performs shared resources management among different active and inactive containers that leads to flexible resource sharing and high compatibility. Docker can also ensure better resource utilization in the shared resource management when there exist some inactive instances. The inactive instances under hypervisor-based virtualization, may occupy the resources allocated to them but consume negligible resources in containerized virtualization. Thus, active instances are allowed by the containerization to use resources that are unused by inactive instances (Janki Bhimani 2017).

CONCLUSION

The analysis shows that virtualization and containerization technologies can be used to solve the tasks of Big Data processing as a mean of deploying specialized software platforms. In this chapter it is analysed the key technologies of virtualization of computing resources used today. Virtualization has been designed to abstract hardware and system resources in order to ensure that multiple operating systems work together on the basis of one physical node. There are several approaches to the implementation of virtualization. Full virtualization is aimed at hardware emulation. Para virtualization requires modification of the virtualized OS and coordination of operations between the virtual OS and the hypervisor. It is observe that though applications perform better on Docker in comparison to VM, this is not generalized for all big data application running in the distributed cloud framework.

REFERENCES

1. Horne, Chris.(2007) "Understanding full virtualization, paravirtualization and hardware assist". In: White paper, VMware Inc ,.

2. Rao K. Thirupathi, Kiran P. Sai, L.S.S.Reddy,(2010) "Energy Efficiency in Data centers   through Virtualization: A Case Study", Global Journal of Computer Science and Technology, Vol. 10 ,Issue 3 (Ver 1.0), pp. 2-6,April

3. Changqing Ji, Daowen Qiu, Uchechukwu Awada, Keqiu Li,(2012) "Big data processing: Big challenges", Journal of Interconnection Networks, DOI: 10.1142/S0219265912500090 ,Vol. 13, Nos. 3 & 4 , pp. 1-19,.

4. Walter Akio Goya, Marcelo Risse de Andrade, Artur Carvalho Zucchi, Nelson Mimura Gonzalez, Rosangela de Fatima Pereira, Karen Langona, Jan-Erik Mangs, Azimeh Sefidcon, (2014)"The Use of Distributed Processing and Cloud Computing in Agricultural Decision-Making Support Systems", IEEE International   Conference   on   Cloud   Computing,   DOI 10.1109/CLOUD.2014.101, pp. 721-728,.

5. Malhotra L, Agarwal D , Jaiswal A , (2014)"Virtualization in Cloud Computing", Journal of Information Technology & Software Engineering", doi:10.4172/2165-7866, Volume 4 , Issue 2,pp. 1-4,.

6. Dua R., A. R. Raja,(2014) and D. Kakadia, "Virtualization vs containerization to support PaaS," in Cloud Engineering (IC2E), 2014 IEEE International Conference on. IEEE, , pp. 610–614.

7. Marisol García-Valls,Tommaso Cucinotta, Chenyang Lu, "Challenges in real-time virtualization and predictable cloud computing", Journal of Systems Architecture, ELSEVIER, http://dx.doi.org/10.1016/j.sysarc.2014.07.004, pp. 1-15, 2014.

8. Rakesh Kumar, Shilpi Charu, " An Importance of using Virtuallization Technology in Cloud Computing", Global Journal of Computers & Technology, Vol. 1, No. 2, February 25, pp. 56-60, 2015.

9. Roberto Morabito, Jimmy Kjällman, and Miika Komu, "Hypervisors vs. Lightweight Virtualization: a Performance Comparison", IEEE International Conference on Cloud Engineering, DOI 10.1109/IC2E.2015.74, pp. 386-393, 2015.

10. Radu F. Babiceanu, Remzi Seker, "Big Data and virtualization for manufacturing cyber-physical systems: A survey of the current status and future outlook", Computers in Industry, ELSEVIER, http://dx.doi.org/10.1016/j.compind.2016.02.004, pp. 1-10, 2016.

11. Janki Bhimani, Zhengyu Yang, Miriam Leeser, and Ningfang Mi, "Accelerating Big Data Applications Using Lightweight Virtualization Framework on Enterprise Cloud", IEEE High Performance Extreme Computing Conference (HPEC), DOI: 10.1109/HPEC.2017.8091086, pp. 1-7, 2017.

12. Sandeepkumar Mathivanana, Prabhu Jayagopal, "Big Data Virtualization Role in Agriculture: A Comprehensive Review", Walailak J Sci & Tech ,16(2), pp. 55-70, 2018.

13. Zaineb t. Al-azez , ahmed q. Lawey, taisir e. H. El-gorashi, jaafar m. H. Elmirghani, "Energy Efficient IoT Virtualization Framework With Peer to Peer Networking and Processing", IEEE Access, Vol 7, pp. 50697- 50709, 2019.

14. Gleb I. Radchenko , Ameer B. A. Alaasam, Andrei N. Tchernykh, "Comparative Analysis of Virtualization Methods in Big Data Processing", ResearchGate, DOI: 10.14529/js_190107, Vol. 6, No. 1, pp. 48-79, 2019.

PREDICTION OF COVID-19 USING ARIMA MODEL

Dr. Mamata Garanayak

Department of Computer Science & Engineering,
Centurion University of Technology and Management,
Odisha, India

INTRODUCTION

The COVID 19 global epidemic, widely identified as corona virus outbreak, is a growing global corona virus disease contagion in 2019 (COVID19), triggered by extreme acute respiratory corona virus syndrome 2 (SARS CoV2) [1]. The epidemic was first recognized in the year 2019 December in city Wuhan, China. The eruption was announced a communal health crisis of international treat by the WHO on 30th January 2020 and a pandemic on 11th March 2020. As of 17th July 2020, more than 13.8 million sufferer of COVID19 have been appeared in more than 188 countries and dominions, proceeding in more than 589,000 passing; more than 7.71 million persons have recuperated [2]. Globally Covid 19 pandemic is now one of the major concerns around the globe. Due to this pandemic the world is going through a tough situation. The world came to a standstill for this pandemic. Round the globe all are facing a tensed situation. Mortality rate and transmission of the disease growing rapidly throughout the world though in some countries it becomes stable. All countries seek to save their lives by enforcing steps such as travel bans, quarantines, postponements and cancellations of activities, social barriers, examinations, hard and soft lockdowns [3]. It has an impact upon the survival of mankind economically and socially. People infected with the virus this face difficulty breathing because of fluid and pus in the lung. This happens because the air sacs swelling in one or both lungs. Covid-19's most ordinary indications covers brittle cough, fever, fatigue, and less ordinary indications covers pains, agonizing throat, diarrhea, headache, mislaying of taste and smell, skin rash, or finger or toe discoloration, trouble breathing or shortness of breath, chest pain, or pressure [4]. So if someone has some of those symptoms, COVID-19 test may be referred to. On July 7 there were 98 192 cumulative cases of infection worldwide and 3,045 deaths have been reported.

Viral wide lay outs are a consequential threat. COVID-19 is not the earliest, and it won't be the rearmost. But, like not at all before, we are gathering and sharing what we grasp about the virus. Hundreds of investigation teams around the world are merging their endeavor to gather data and evolve solutions. We want to radiate brightness on their efforts and show how machine learning is helping us to [5]:

- Forecast the proliferation of the infection,

- Identify sufferer

- Evolve medicines quickly

- Forecast the succeeding broad extend.

Machine learning is a foremost tool in contest to the current wide layout. If we take this moment to gather information, puddle our grasp, and merge our expertise, we can rescue so many human beings – both at the moment and in later also. The leading neutral of this paper is to forecast 7 days ahead COVID-19 prediction of different countries by Auto-ARIMA Time Series Forecasting model.

RELATED WORK

For COVID-19's recent research and development and its effects, several researchers have developed specific prediction models based on data. Corona virus extend is not an ideal aggressive unfurl, because of which the traditional epidemiological method utilized to prototype extend of infectious sickness does not describe the COVID 19. Many researchers applied machine learning algorithms for better prediction. Few are cited below.

The literature includes several articles on forecasting infectious diseases. The method of Auto Regressive Integrated Moving Average (ARIMA) is also used to forecast time-series. The reason it's so widely used is because it can get useful statistical properties. They are also very flexible, as they can represent multiple time series using different parameters of order. Many diseases, such as Hemorrhagic Fever with Renal Syndrome (HFRS], Brucellosis, Influenza, and COVID-19, were predicted using the ARIMA approach.

Petropoulos F. & Makridakis S.- 2020 [6] describes the time line of a populate prediction exertion with enormous huge suggestions for organization and conclusion building and imparts unbiased predictions for the sure occurrences of COVID 19. They feel that prediction and their related uncertainty should be a basic lump of the conclusion building operation, mainly in hazard instances. Besides the notable communal health examine, the hazard forced on global furnish chains and the wealth as an entire are as well countable. Risk-averse human beings can aim on the worst-case-framework and take action suitably. Determining to exclude any approved, statistical predictions and taking action, still oblique an underlying predicting procedure, even if this procedure is not formalized. Here, they utilized time series prototypes, which presume that the data is correct and previously patterns consisting of precautionary measures will continue to put in. Significant, congruous prediction errors such as dynamically spanning outer to the predict interim should be related with changes in noticed patterns and the requirement for additional activity and measures in the instance of negatively influenced predictions.

Salgotra R., Gandomi M. & Gandomi A. H. – 2020 [7] presented the work where the forecast prototypes relied on genetic programming have been evolved for sure instances and passing instanced across 3 most overripe states such as Gujarat, Maharashtra and Delhi as well as throughout the India. The suggested prediction prototypes are dispensed by utilizing explicit formula and the importance of forecast variables is examined. For developed and validate the prototypes, the statistical variables and metrics have been utilized. From the outcomes, it has been established that the suggested GEP-relied prototypes use easy linkage functions and are really trustable for time series forecasting of COVID 19 instances in India.

In this paper a vigorous and trusted variant of GEP was utilized to mock-up the positive instances and passing instances of COVID 19 (India). New right factual prototypes were planned for forecast of positive instances and passing instances across entire India and 3 crucial states which are severely overripe by the COVID 19 widespread. These states consist of Maharashtra, Gujarat and Delhi. The suggested prototypes were evolved from the day-to-day circumstances arrive of COVID-19 instances reported by the Ministry of Home Affairs.

Huang C., Wang Y., Li X., Ren L., Zhao J., Hu Y., Zhang L., Fan G., Xu J. & Gu X. – 2020 [8] announce the hygienic, clinical, laboratory, and radiometric features and therapy and clinical results of the sufferers. They gathered and inspected information on sufferers with laboratory sure 2019-nCoV contamination by RT-PCR (real time) and further-cohort sequencing. Information was procured with normalized information gathering forms circulated by health organization and the International Severe Acute Respiratory and Emerging Infection Consortium reports. Researchers consult with sufferers face to face or their households to ascertain hygienic and manifestation data. Results were also contrasted among sufferers who had been confessing to the intensive care unit and also those who had not admitted.

Chaurasia V. & Pal S. – 2020 [9] carried out a study on Corona virus to notice the number of occurrences, passing and healing instances worldwide within a particular period of time that is 5 months. Relied on this data, this article forecasts the succeeding unfurl of this contagious illness in human community. In this paper, they took the data set of "Data WHO Corona virus Covid-19 cases and deaths-WHO-COVID-19-global-data". This information set consist the data regarding the date of observation, state, country and up to date updates. In this paper, they executed different prediction methodologies such as naive technique, moving average, simple average, single exponential smoothing, Holt linear trend technique, Holt Winter technique and ARIMA, for comparison, and how these techniques revamp the Root mean square error outcome. They established that the naive technique is fitted best as explained over all other techniques. In the ARIMA technique, using grid search, they found a lot of walls that conveyed the best-fit technique for their time series information. By continuing the prototype, succeeding forecast of passing away instances specify that the number of passing away will be increased by more than 600,000 by January 2020. They conclude that this research will assist the Govt. and researchers in building arrangements for what is going to occur. Depending on the results of instantaneous techniques, these prototypes can be fitted to guide long time.

Mandal M., Jana S., Nandi S.K., Khatua A., Adak S., & Kar T.K. – 2020 [10] have composed a mathematical prototype by establishing a quarantine category and governmental interference quantify to take the edge off infection channeling. They examine an in-depth rigorous characteristics of the prototype in phrases of the fundamental copying number.

Additionally, they carry out the sensitivity inspection of the required copying number and establish that lessening the contact of reveal and permitting community is the most crucial element in attaining infection domination. To minimize the infected persons as well as to lessen the economy of implementing government control strategies, they developed an optimal control problem, and also determine the optimal control. At last, they predict a short term fashion of COVID 19 for the three towering contaminated states (Maharashtra, Delhi, and Tamil Nadu) in India, and it recommends that the first 2 states require additional investigation of control strategies to lessen the contact of reveal and permitting community.

Fanelli D., & Piazza F. – 2020 [11] examine the secular dynamics of the corona virus infection 2019 upsurge in China, Italy and France in the accent window 22/01/2020–15/03/2020 and 22/01/2020-15/03/2020 respectively. An earliest examination of easy day-lag maps points to some universality in the infection unfurl, proposing that easy mean area prototypes can be successfully utilized to collect an assessable image of the infection unfurl, and above all the height and time of the crest of sure infected persons. The examination of the data within a simple susceptible-infected-recovered-deaths prototype specifies that the active parameter that narrates the rate of recuperation seems to be the same, no matter what is the country, while the unfurl and passing away rates pop up to be more variable. The prototype spots the crest in Italy near around March 23rd, with a crest number of infected persons of near around 26100 were recovered and passing away cases are not included and a number of passing away at the end of the unfurl of near around 18,300. Since the confirmed instances are believed to be between 11% and 21% of the real number of persons who eventually get infected, the obvious impermanence rate of COVID 19 drops between 3.9% and 8.2% in Italy, while it pop up considerably lower, between 1.2% and 3.1% in China. Depending on their calculations, they calculate that 2510 ventilation units should represent impartial particulars for the pop up requirement to be considered by health administrations in Italy for their planning. Ultimately, a simulation of the results of high containment criteria on the eruption in Italy specifies that a cutting of the unfurl rate indeed causes a quench of the unfurl pop up.

PROPOSED APPROACH

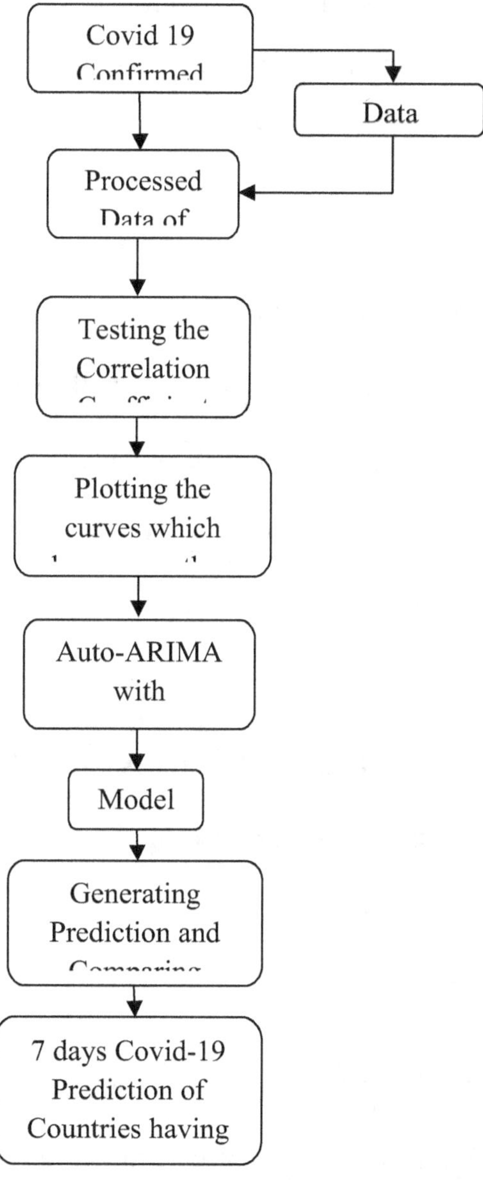

FIGURE 1: Proposed Approach

The proposed approach is shown in Figure 1. In the suggested approach, the Time Series Forecasting Techniques is used to build a model which comes up with seven days ahead predictions of confirmed cases of COVID-19 in India. System is assembled in following phases such as collection of data sets, pre-processing phases, testing the correlation and plotting the curves which have more than 90% correlation and less than 100 MSE. After that it find the exogenous variable and target variable to fit the ARIMA model for generating the prediction and comparing actual versus forecast data frame and finally predicts the 7 days Covid-19 prediction of the different countries having best coefficient correlation between growth curves.

COLLECTION OF DATA SETS AND PRE-PROCESSING STEP

Collection or gathering of data is the procedure of collecting and quantifying information from innumerable several origins. In order to utilize the data, we collect to expand practical forecast solutions, it must be gathered and deposited in a manner that creates sense for the prediction problem at hand. The Data for the forecasting of COVID-19 for the next 7 days in India is collected from covid19india.org – Corona virus Eruption in India and Ministry of Health and Family Welfare.

In machine learning, this phase is a very crucial phase. Pre-processing of Covid-19 instances data consists of transforming Raw Covid-19 Data day-wise into understandable format by grouping the Covid-19 instances according to state-wise so that we can explore the Data. But for fitting into ARIMA model and for Predictions, data must be in Time Series.

Testing the Correlation Coefficient between Growth Curves

The number of confirmed cases of different countries are considered to test the correlation coefficient between growth curves.

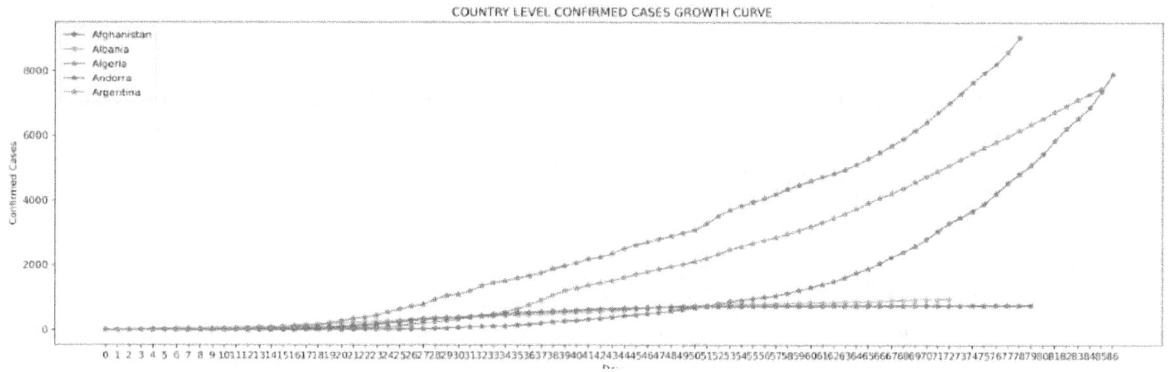

COUNTRY LEVEL CONFIRMED CASES GROWTH CURVE

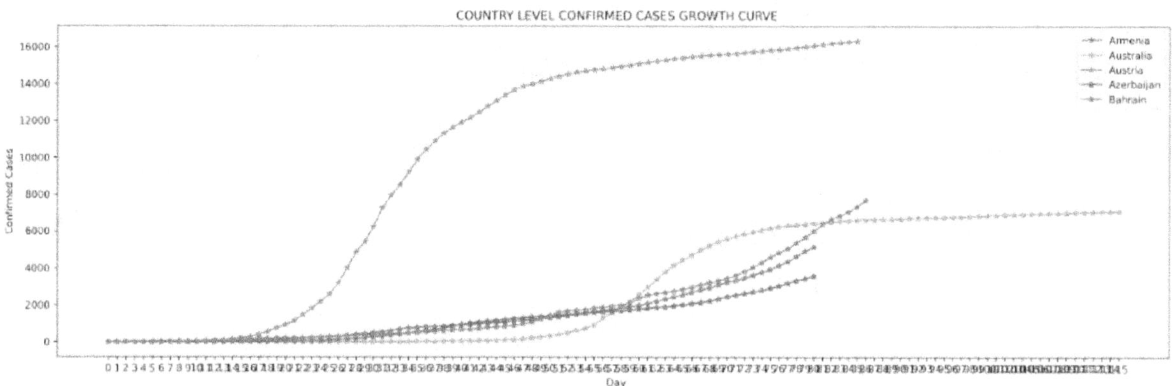

COUNTRY LEVEL CONFIRMED CASES GROWTH CURVE

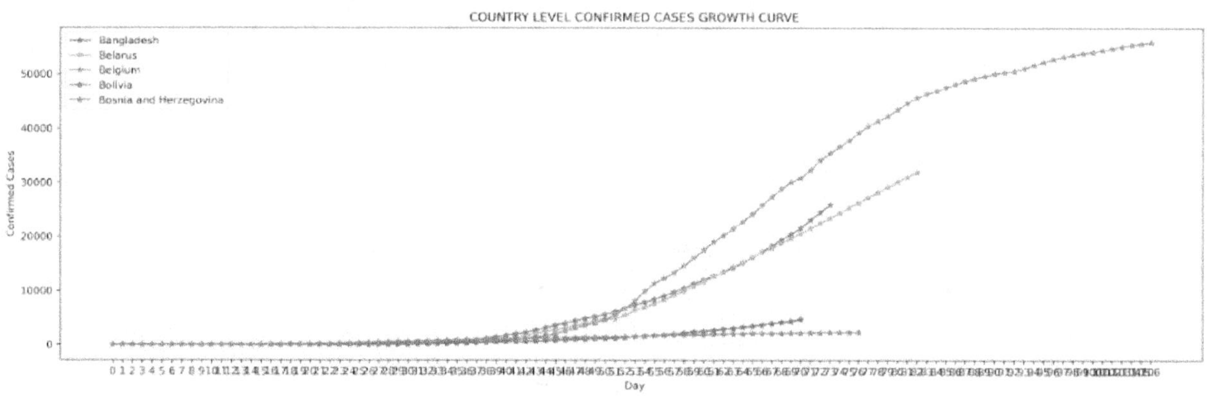

COUNTRY LEVEL CONFIRMED CASES GROWTH CURVE

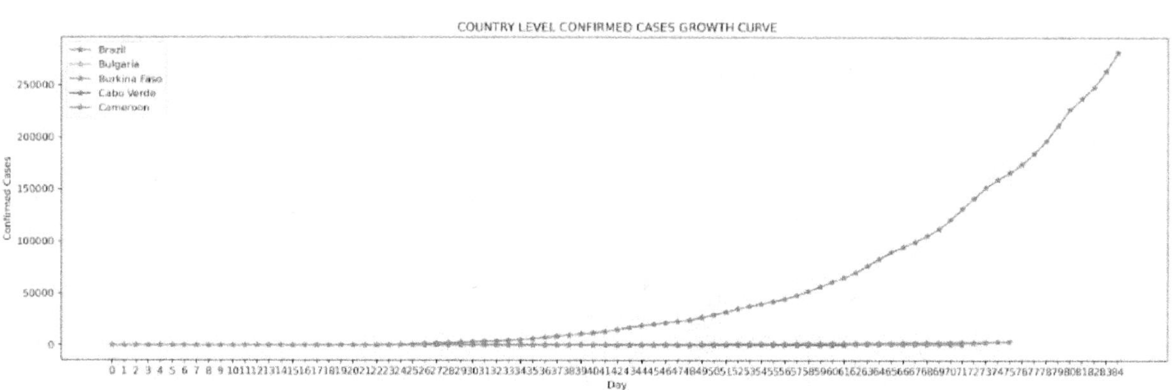

COUNTRY LEVEL CONFIRMED CASES GROWTH CURVE

FIGURE 2: Correlation Coefficient between Growth Curves

Testing the Coefficient Correlation between Growth Curves and plotting the curves which have More than 90% Correlation and Less than 100 MSE

Here there is an attempt to find the correlation and mean square distance between the curves and then selecting the curves which have highest correlation more than 90% and MSE less than 100. This gives information within US states how the cases are increasing with time. With this approach we can utilize the growth rate available from past experience to forecast future risk. Some correlation results are given in Figure 3.

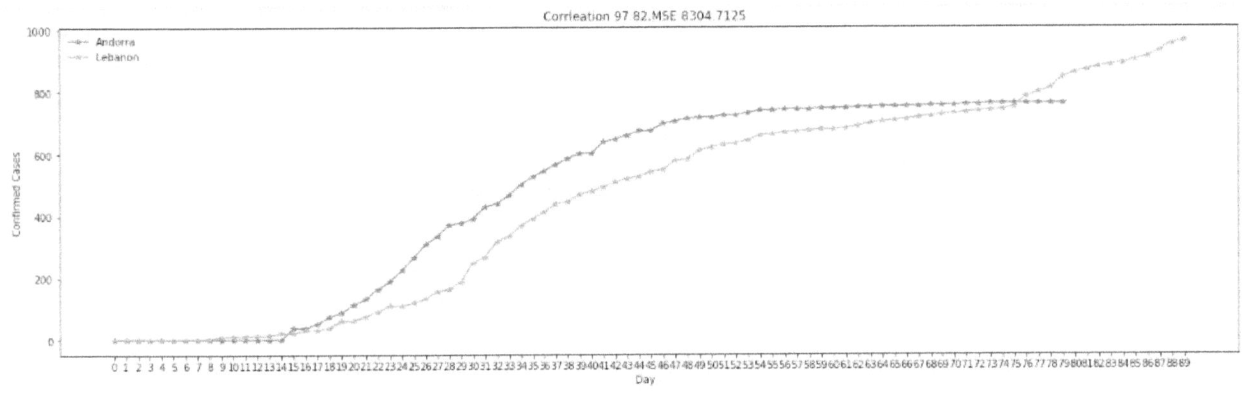

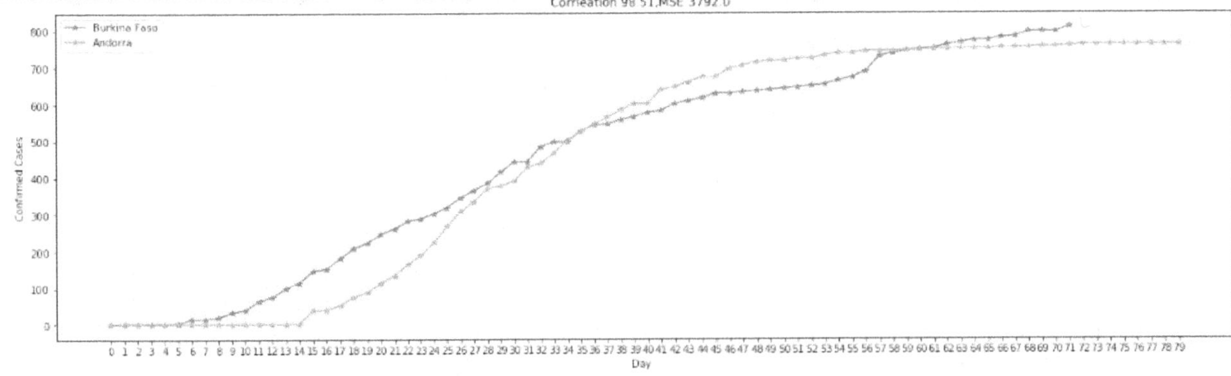

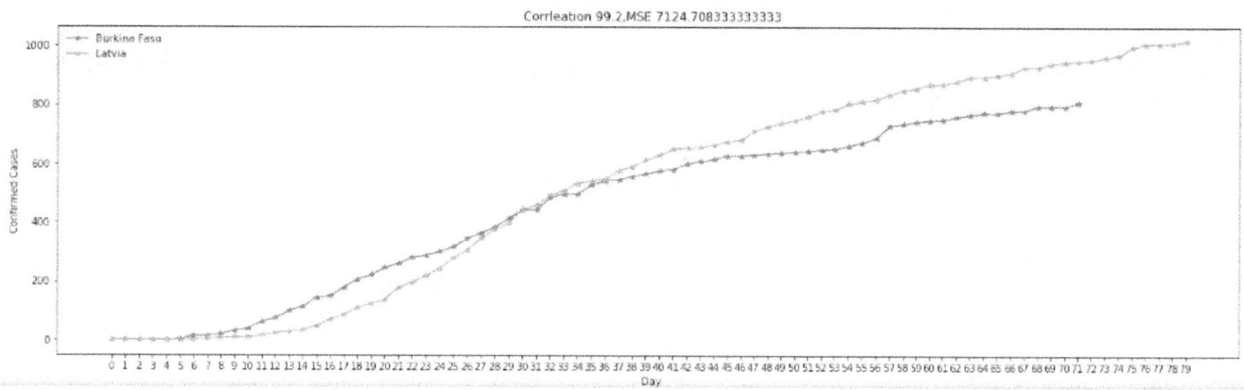

Corrleation 99.2,MSE 7124.708333333333

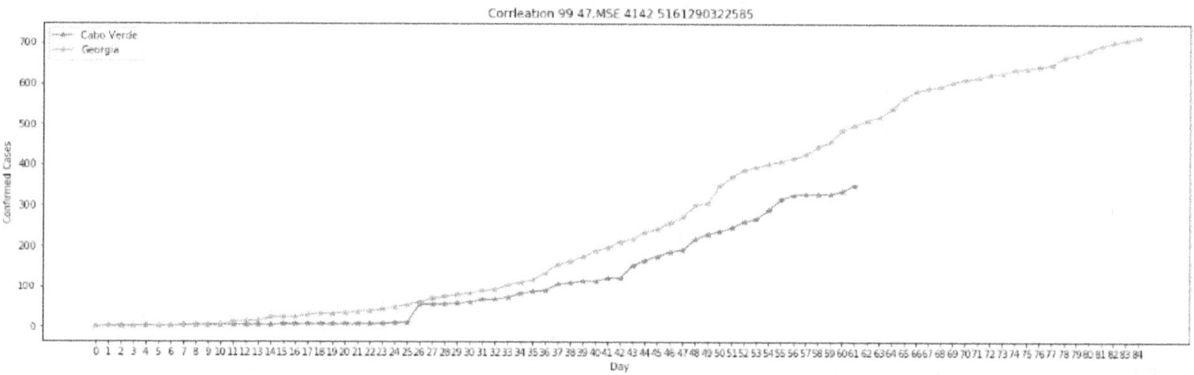

Corrleation 99.47,MSE 4142.5161290322585

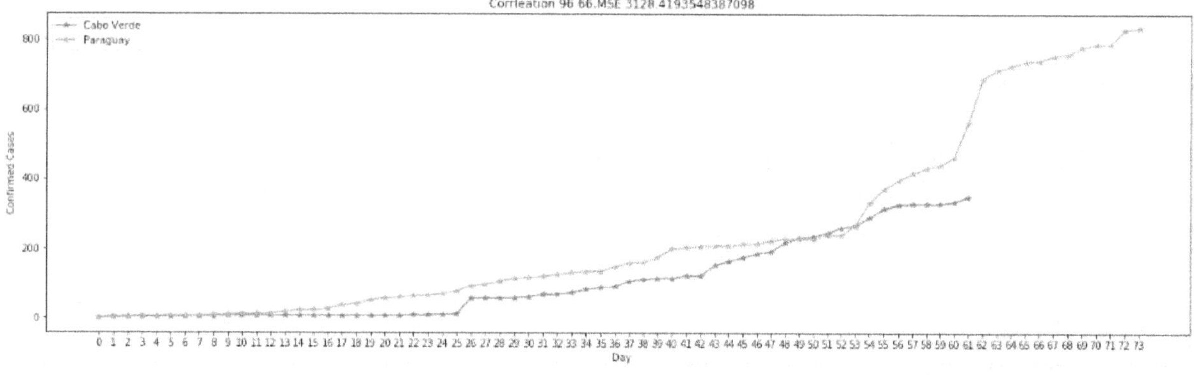

Corrleation 96.66,MSE 3128.4193548387098

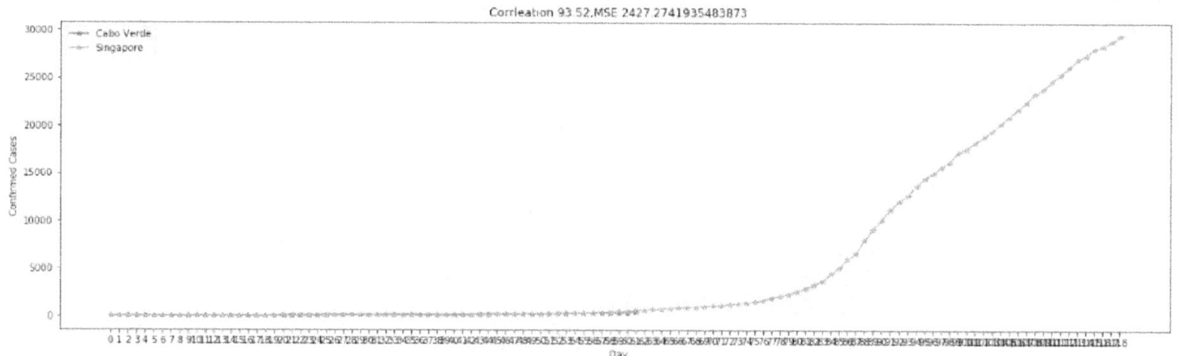

Corrleation 93.52,MSE 2427.2741935483873

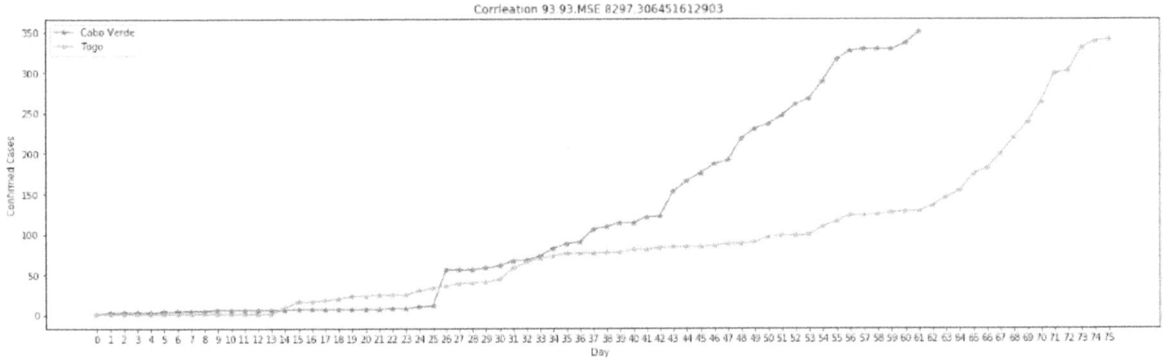

FIGURE 3: Curves which have more than 90% correlation and less than 100 MSE

Auto-ARIMA with EXOGENOUS Variable and Target Variable

```
[  1   1   1   1   1   1   1   1   1   1   1   1   1   2  39  39  53
  75  88 113 133 164 188 224 267 308 334 370 376 390 428 439 466 501 525
 545 564 583 601 601 638 646 659 673 673 696 704 713 717 717 723 723 731
 738 738 743 743 743 745 745 747 748 750 751 751 752 752 754 755 755 758
 760 761 761 761 761 761 761 762]
```

Generating Prediction

```
forecast [765.57992114 762.2073109  768.05340755 775.076453   782.47259992
 785.05423657 796.71785118] confidence interval [[750.38981834 780.77002395]
 [737.99703406 786.41758773]
 [735.09618296 801.01063214]
 [733.27101635 816.88188965]
 [731.63445184 833.310748  ]
 [725.02421955 845.08425359]
 [727.31494523 866.12075714]]
```

Actual Vs Forecast Data Frame

	Actuals	Ci_high	Ci_low	forecast
77	761.0	NaN	NaN	NaN
78	761.0	NaN	NaN	NaN
79	762.0	NaN	NaN	NaN
80	NaN	780.770024	750.389818	765.579921
81	NaN	786.417588	737.997034	762.207311
82	NaN	801.010632	735.096183	768.053408
83	NaN	816.881890	733.271016	775.076453
84	NaN	833.310748	731.634452	782.472600
85	NaN	845.084254	725.024220	785.054237
86	NaN	866.120757	727.314945	796.717851

7 Days Covid-19 Prediction of Countries having Best Coefficient Correlation between Growth Curves

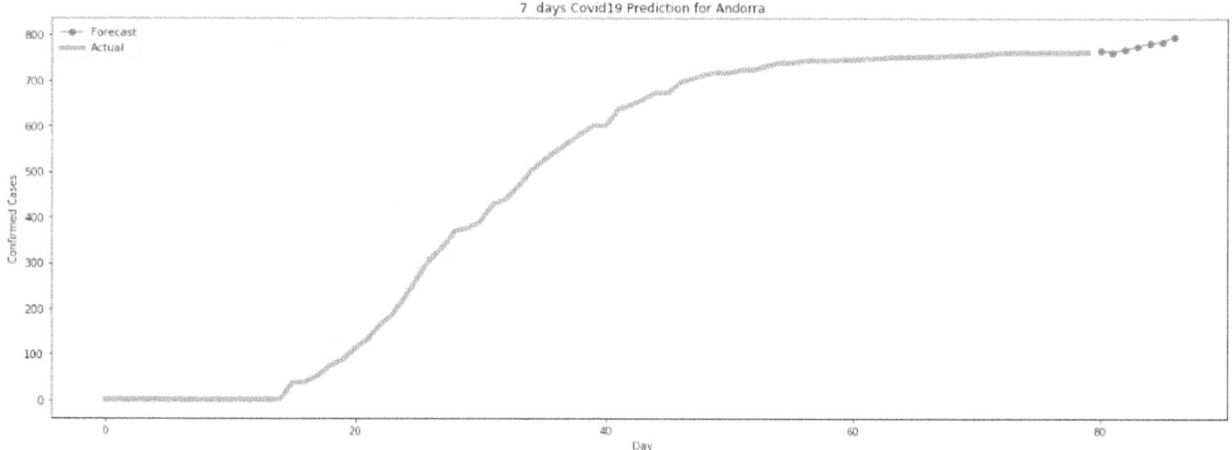

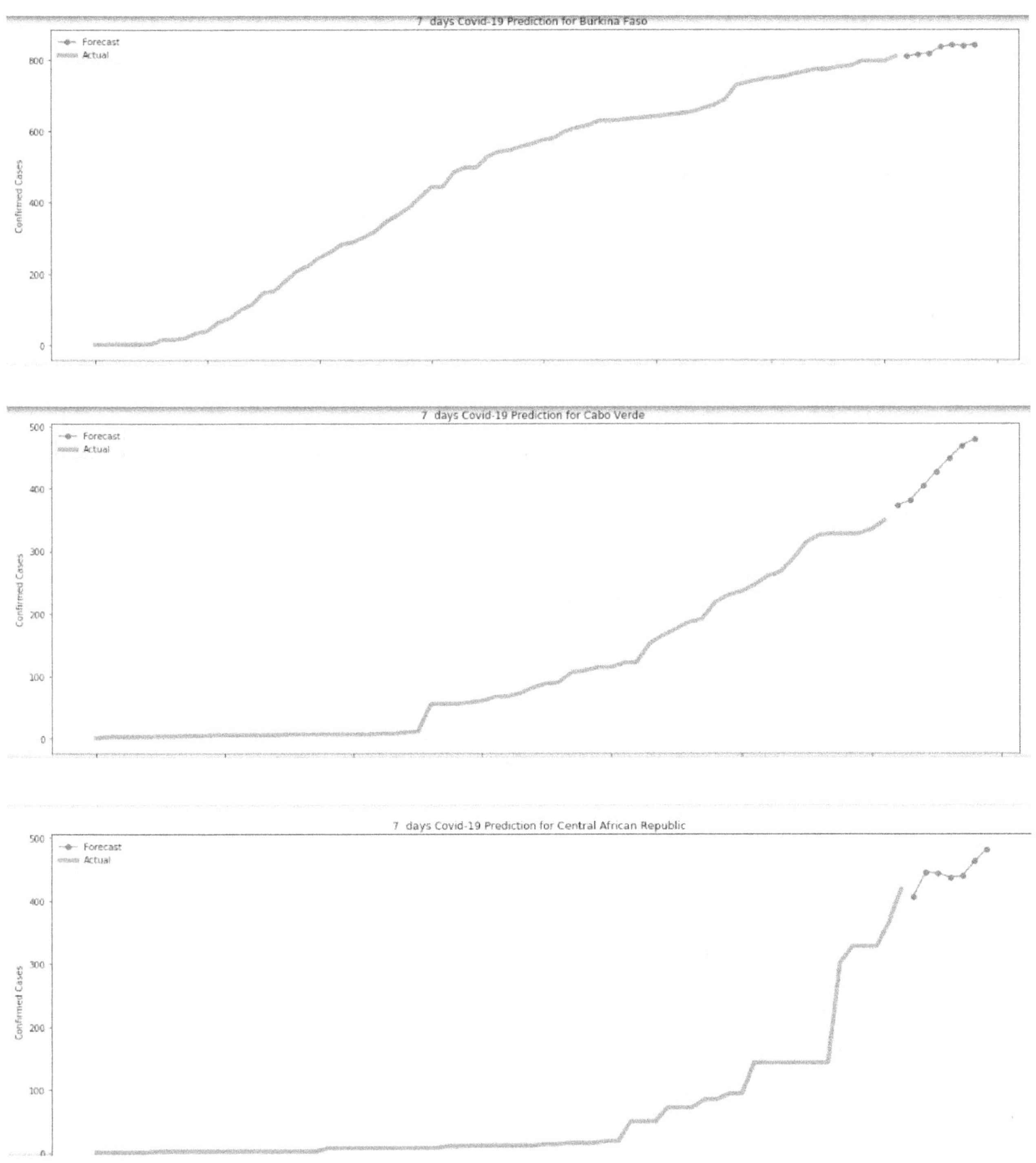

FIGURE 4: 7 Days Covid-19 Prediction of some countries

4. CONCLUSION AND FUTURE WORK

In this chapter, an information-driven Auto-ARIMA prototype has been utilized to find the possible number of positive instances of Covid 19 in India for the succeeding 7 days ahead. The number of daily positive instances has also been estimated. The consequence of preventing considers such as isolation (social) and lockdown has also been examined which manifests that by these preventive categories, extend of the virus can be reduced. The forecasted outcomes from the prototypes could differ in a significant way from the perceived ones, if there is a change in the imminent days due to several testing schemes, social distancing strategies, re-opening the faction, or stay home strategy, the forecasted passing away instances will surely differ. Undeniably, additional examinations in validation of this ending are required by improving the actual present day COVID 19 data into the prototype.

REFERENCES

[1] Covid19india.org: Corona virus Eruption in India. Government of India (2020). Accessed fromhttps://www.covid19india.org/ on 13th June 2020.

[2] John Hopkins University (2020). Novel Corona Virus (COVID-19) Instances, provided by JHU CSSE. Accessed from https://github.com/CSSEGISand Data/COVID-19.

[3] Gupta, R., Pandey, G., Chaudhary, P., & Pal, S. K. (2020). SEIR and Regression Model based COVID-19 eruption predictions in India. Accessed from https://www.medrxiv.org/content/10.1101/2020.04.01.20049825.

[4] World Health Organization (2020). Corona virus infection (COVID-19) Wide spread, WHO. Accessed from https://www.who.int/emergencies/infections/ novel-coronavirus-2019.

[5] The Ministry of Health and Family Welfare (MoHFW), Government of India (2020) Corona virus infection (COVID-19) Wide spread. Accessed from https://www.mohfw.gov.in/ on 13th June 2020.

[6] Petropoulos F., & Makridakis S. (2020). Forecasting the novel coronavirus COVID-19. Plos One, accessed from https://doi.org/10.1371/journal.pone.0231236, 15(3): 1-8.

[7] Salgotra R., Gandomi M., & Gandomi A. H. (2020). Time Series Analysis and Forecast of the COVID-19 Pandemic in India using Genetic Programming. Elsevier Public Health Emergency Collection, accessed from https://www.ncbi.nlm.nih.gov/pmc/articles/PMC7260529/.

[8] Huang C., Wang Y., Li X., Ren L., Zhao J., Hu Y., Zhang L., Fan G., Xu J., & Gu X. Clinical features of patients infected with 2019 novel coronavirus in wuhan. China Lancet. 2020; 395: 497–506.

[9] Chaurasia V., & Pal S. Covid-19 Pandemic: Application of Machine Learning Time Series Analysis for Prediction of Human Future, research article Biomedical engineering, accessed from https://www.researchsquare.com/article/rs-39149/v1.

[10] Mandal M., Jana S., Nandi S.K., Khatua A., Adak S., & Kar T.K. A model based study on the dynamics of COVID-19: Prediction and control. Chaos, Solitons & Fractals. 2020:109889.

[11] Fanelli D., Piazza F. Analysis and forecast of COVID-19 spreading in China, Italy and France. Chaos Solitons Fractals. 2020; 134:109761.

NEED FOR MACHINE LEARNING IN SMART AGRICULTURE

Rakesh Kumar Ray
Department of Computer Science
Centurion University of Technology and Management
Odisha, India

INTRODUCTION

Food is the basic need for all living things and agriculture is the critical and important sector to fulfilling the basic needs of the whole world. It is the main source of food for the human race. However, agriculture has its own challenges to produce better quality and more quantity, considering factors like reducing environmental degradation, the use of natural resources, and frequent change of climate in the present time. So, it is become very essential to change from the traditional method of agriculture to modern agriculture. Smart agriculture is one of the solutions to meet the challenge of fulfilling the growing demand for food demands. The role of information is vital in the case of smart agriculture. Information like weather condition, diseases, insects, soil parameters, fertilizers, irrigation, etc. are important factures that contribute to production which leads to the economic and sustainable development. Management of all this information for decision making on agriculture and accurate prediction of crops requires systematic and vigilant steps. The steps are like collection, transformation, selection, and analysis of data. The increase of information in agriculture was forced to introduce robust analytical techniques. The machine learning is gratifying the need for managing massive real-time data analysis in smart agriculture[1].

According to the Department of Economics and Social Affairs, United Nation, report published on 21 June 2017, the approximately 83 million people are being added every year to the world's population and estimated to reach 8.6 billion and 9.8 billion, respectively, in

2030 and 2050 and 11.2 billion in 2100 [2]. So, the world food production needs to increase by 50% to feed the growing human population demand for food. It is very essential to change the agriculture production procedure and adopt modern techniques and technologies.

Smart agriculture is the process of the use of data collected through sources (geographical, historical, and instrumental) and analyzes the data to implement in the management of farm activities. The smart agriculture includes weather analysis and prediction, manage firm zones through satellite image, analyze soil data to predict suitable crops, irrigation management, early detection of plant diseases to increase the productivity of cultivation.

IoT plays a crucial role in the collection of data from the field to processing. IoT in agriculture includes drones, sensors, and robots that are connected through the internet. These may be automatic or semi-automatic to gather data. Smart agriculture is a solution to the shortage of labor across the globe.

The absence of machine learning or data mining in smart agriculture cannot be imagined. Machine learning is the brain of smart agriculture that analyzes the collected data through IoT for decision making[3]. The applications of machine learning in agriculture are Species Breeding, Species Recognition, Soil management, Water Management, Yield Prediction, Crop Quality, Disease Detection, Weed Detection, etc.

MACHINE LEARNING

"Machine Learning is defined as the study of computer programs that leverage algorithms and statistical models to learn through inference and patterns without being explicitly programmed. Machine Learning field has undergone significant developments in the last decade"1. Machine learning algorithm is based on mathematical modeling of training data to

---

1 https://www.toolbox.com/tech/artificial-intelligence/tech-101/what-is-machine-learning-definition-types-applications-and-examples/ by Anirudh V K dt- December 13, 2019

predict or classify which can be used for decision making without explicitly programmed to do so. It can be classified into 3 categories. Supervised Learning, Unsupervised Learning, and Reinforcement Learning.

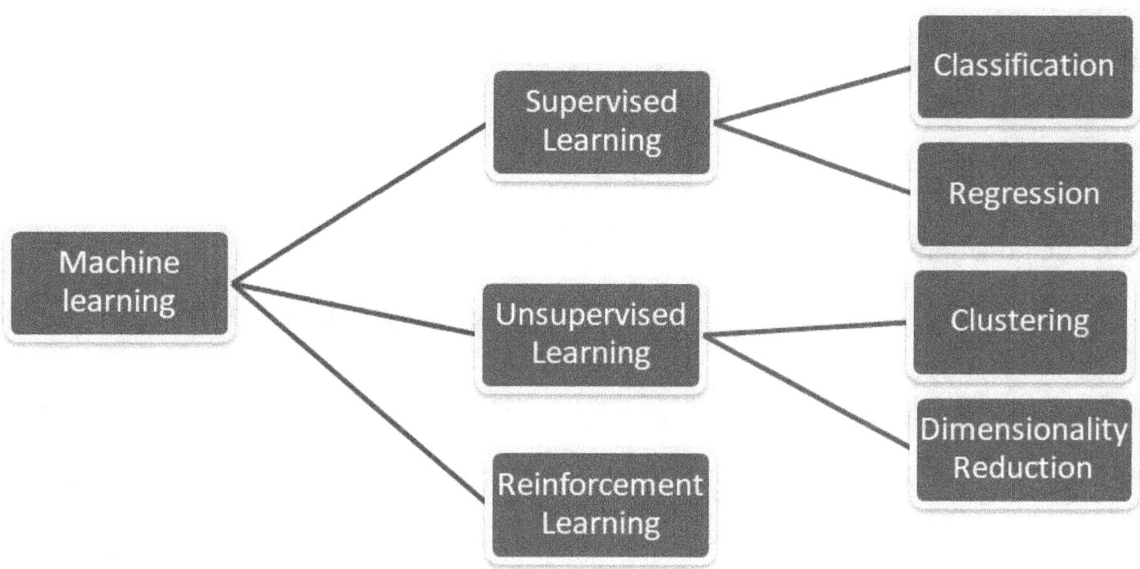

FIGURE1 Types of Machine Learning

Supervised Learning: The supervised learning applied to leveled data[4], where every input has its output. The algorithm derives a mathematical relationship between the input and output to predict the output of new input. The prediction can be either regression (estimate continuous value) or classification (identify unique class).

Unsupervised Learning: The unsupervised learning applied to unleveled data, where supplied input has no output. The goal of an unsupervised learning algorithm is to discover the hidden patterns. Clustering and dimensionality reduction are done using unsupervised learning[5].

Reinforcement Learning (RL): Reinforcement learning is a type of machine learning technique that enables an agent to learn in an interactive environment by trial and error using feedback from its own actions and experiences

MACHINE LEARNING TECHNIQUES

There are various machine learning techniques. In this chapter, a few popular techniques have been discussed.

Artificial Neural Network

ANN's computational process imitates the human brain's biological operation. It can build a complex nonlinear relationship between input and output[6]. It has three layers, input layer, hidden layer, and output layer. The input layer is used to pass data from the outside world to the model. The number of neurons depend upon the input variable (independent variables). The output layer transfers information from the model to the outside world. The hidden layer performs all computational work, which is an intermediate layer between the input layer and the output layer. ANN is one of the popular techniques for many researchers. ANN is being used for predicting accurate paddy yield[7].

Support Vector Machine

Support vector machines (SVMs) are popular and flexible supervised learning algorithms that are used both for regression and classification. An SVM model is a representation of classes in a hyperplane in multidimensional space. The hyperplane is generated iteratively by SVM to minimized error. The goal of SVM is to find a maximum marginal hyperplane by dividing the datasets into classes. In the model [8] rice yield has been predicted using the Indian dataset and SVM is used for Prediction of Wheat Stripe Rust in the paper[9].

K-Nearest Neighbors (KNN)

KNN is a simple machine learning technique that can be used for classification and regression problems. This has no training phase while the prediction of new targets uses all training data. It applies distance function (eg. Minkowski, Manhattan, Euclidean distance function) to compute the distance from a new input predictor to all training predictors, and then k nearest distances are nominated with corresponding target values. It works on the locality concept and it is used for nonlinear and highly adaptable problems. KNN time and space complexity are comparably higher than other machine learning techniques as it uses all data during the prediction of new data case. In the paper [10] K-NN has been implemented to distinguish among stress types using field image.

Decision Tree Learning

A decision tree is a supervised learning algorithm used for both classification and regression. The decision tree is based on tree, which split the sample space recursively into smaller sub-sample space on condition that is formulated by a model that can predict the output. The internal node represents attribute (feature), the branches represent decision rules and each leaf node is the output. It is a top-to-down approach. There are many algorithms built on decision trees namely CART, M5, and M5-Prime. In the paper[11] author has implemented m5prime to predict crop yield.

Random Forest

Random forest is a supervised learning method that operates a number of decision trees on several subsets of the given dataset and the final decision is made based on the majority vote of prediction on decision trees which improve the predictive accuracy of that dataset. In the paper [12] random forest analysis is being implemented for soil organic carbon which gives higher accurate results.

K-Means clustering

K-means clustering is one of the unsupervised algorithms where the available input data does not have a labeled response. K-means clustering is an iterative algorithm that divides a group of data holding m values into k sub-groups. Each of them value fits the k cluster with the nearest mean. In the paper [13], the author has implemented k-means and PSO to extra-green image segmentation. First using k-means the image pixels are clustered and using POS positioning of the particle is done and again using k-means it has been re-calculated.

RELATED WORK

The paper [14] proposed an irrigation model that contains the following components: the Support Vector Regression method forecast solar energy using Solar Energy Prediction, estimates the amount of time and energy needed to execute the next operation, and reduces the irrigation cost using on-demand scheduling optimization. The system uses the TUP (Time of Use Price) model and hourly NWP (Numerical Weather Prediction). The result showed that the payback cost can be reduced by 25.34% and energy and water resources can be saved by 7.97% in comparison with the irrigation method based on soil moisture.

The author [15] proposed an agricultural management model to predict rice yields which need simple and precise estimation techniques in the planning process. The necessity of the study was to evaluate the performance of the ANN model relative to variations of developmental parameters, find whether ANN models which could efficiently predict rice yield in the mountainous region climatic conditions, and compare the effectiveness of ANN models with multiple linear regression models. This paper describes the artificial neural network models as a replacement and a more perfect technique for yield prediction.

Veenadhari et al. [16] proposed a model to predict the influence of climatic parameters namely temperature, evapotranspiration, relative humidity, precipitation used the Decision Tree method on soybean productivity. They have used the ID3 algorithm on two assumptions and established that relative humidity is the most influential parameter on yield, tailed by temperature and precipitation and that the Decision Tree was fast in execution.

In the paper [17] authors have proposed a model using deep neural network (DNN), that took benefit of state-of-the-art modeling and solution techniques that own the Syngenta Crop Challenge award. The model has got a higher prediction accuracy of the average yield, with a root-mean-square-error being 12% and 50% of the standard deviation using predicted weather data for the validation dataset. As per the authors, the RMSE may reduce to 46% of the standard deviation and 11% of the average yield with perfect weather data.

RESEARCH METHOD

Andra Pradesh essentially depends on agriculture. Its population is 7.4% of the population of India. It is the main rice-producing state in India and it's 70% population depends on cultivation. Andhra Pradesh falls in the Agro Climatic Zone-X which is called "Southern Plateau and Hills Region"[2].

The implementation of the machine learning model includes some basic steps namely 1. Collection of data and preprocessing data 2. Selection of model 3. Splitting data into training and testing set 4. Trained the model using training set 5. Test the model using the testing set and 6. Evaluation of model.

TABLE 1. Data Set

---

[2] https://farmech.dac.gov.in/FarmerGuide/AP/index1.html#:~:text=The%20state%20of%20Andhra%20Pradesh%20is%20largely%20dependent%20in%20Agriculture,India's%20main%20rice%20producing%20states.&text=Andhra%20Pradesh%20falls%20in%20the,Southern%20Plateau%20and%20Hills%20Region%E2%80%9D.

	State	District	Crop	Year	Season	Area	Production	Yield
0	ANDHRA PRADESH	ADILABAD	Rice	1998-99	Kharif	66400	152300	2.293675
1	ANDHRA PRADESH	ADILABAD	Rice	1998-99	Rabi	12200	33500	2.745902
2	ANDHRA PRADESH	ADILABAD	Rice	1999-00	Kharif	66388	162451	2.446993
3	ANDHRA PRADESH	ADILABAD	Rice	1999-00	Rabi	10980	26616	2.424044
4	ANDHRA PRADESH	ADILABAD	Rice	2000-01	Kharif	70645	146235	2.069998

The dataset has been collected from the Government of India website. It contains rice production of AP state for 23 states both for Rabi and Kharif. The dataset contains 8 attributes as reflected in Table1. The attribute state and crop is common to all record so it has not been considered for analysis as it is not going to contribute for prediction. The district is a categorical data converted into numerical data. The dataset is divided into two parts as per season that is the type of rice production because it depends upon the rice type production matter. To check the correlation among attributes heatmap and pairplot are used in Figures 2 and 3.

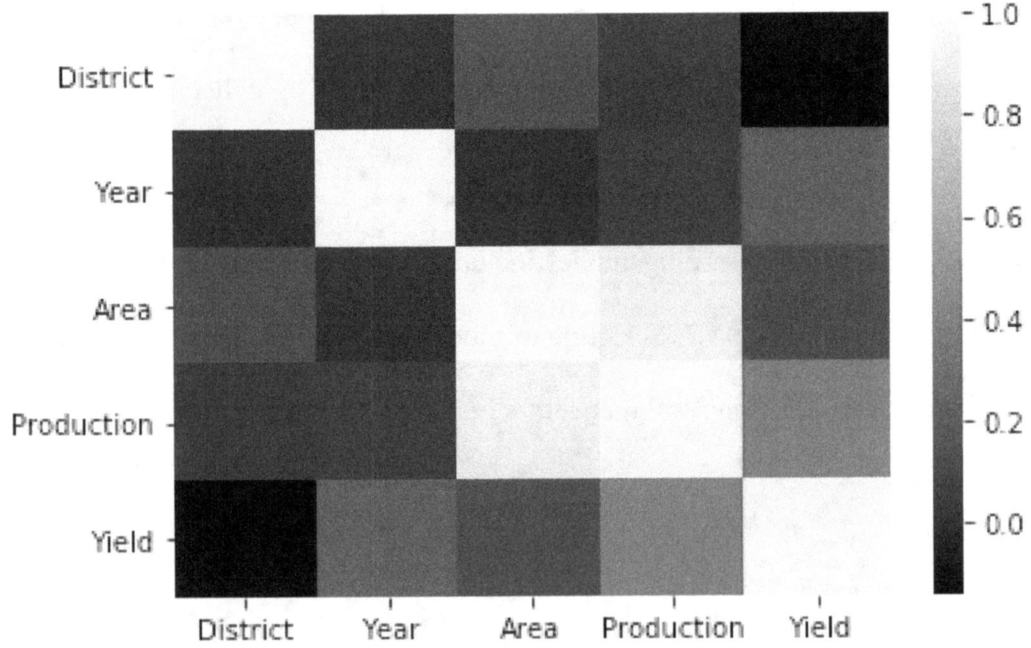

FIGURE 2: Heatmap on the Kharip Rice dataset

Lighter color represents attributes that are correlated.

Heatmap and pairplot has been used for visualization of data. It is clearly observed that the district has very less correlation with yield. Whereas production and year are more correlated respectively to yield.

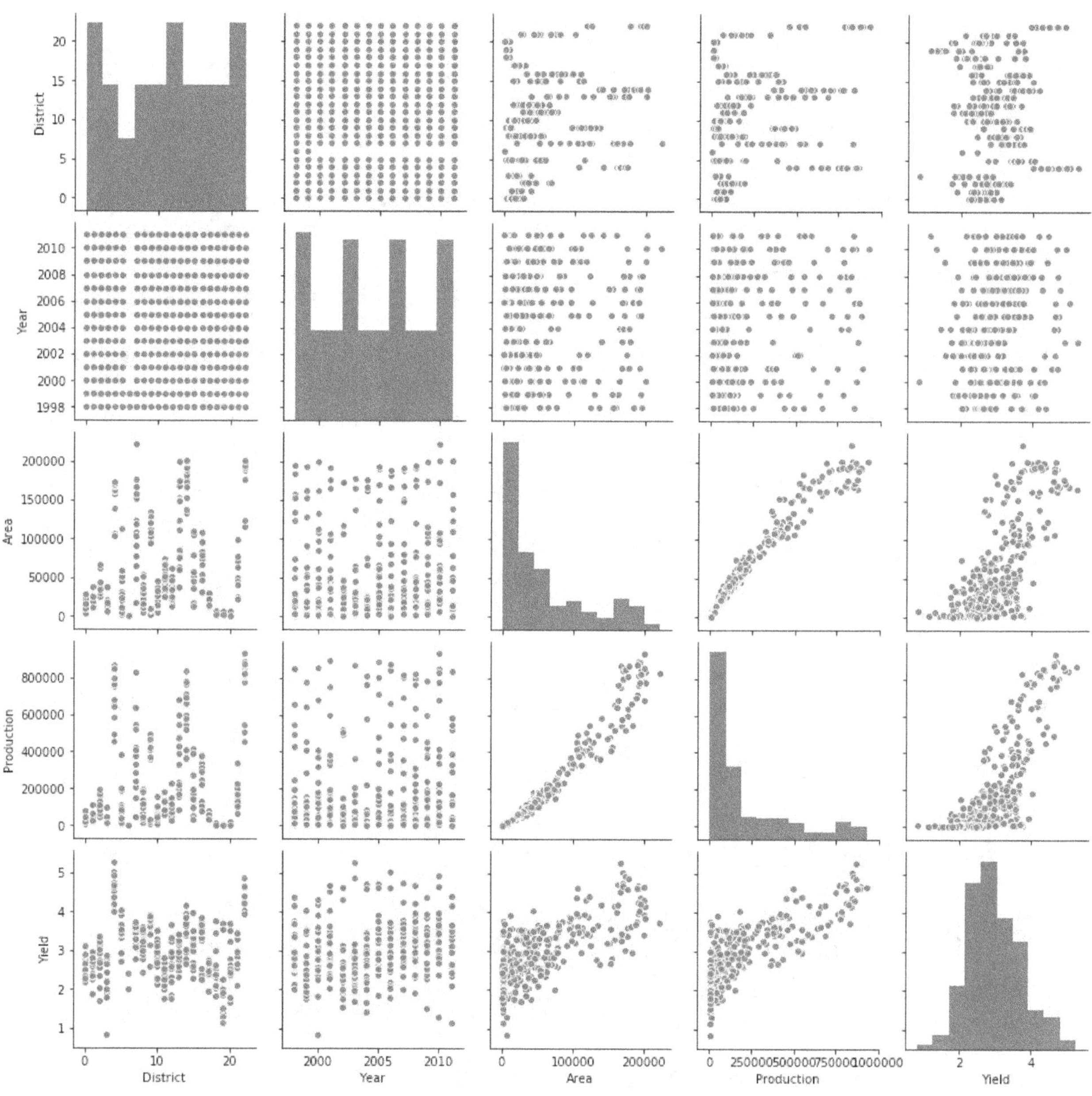

FIGURE 3. Pairplot rabi rice dataset

In this work, the third machine learning algorithm was used to select the model. Those are linear regression, support vector regression, and neural network. The Kharif and Rabi dataset is divided into two sets that are independent and dependent variables. So, the attributes district, year, area, and production have become independent variables and yield the dependent variable.

Now the datasets have been split into training and testing set. There is no specific rule on how the split is to be done. But in general practice, the training set may keep between 70% to 80% and the testing set may keep between 30% to 20%. In this case, the training set has been kept at 80% and the testing set at 20%.

The Linear Regression (LR) and Support Vector Regression (SVR) is used for prediction of yield from rice dataset using the sklearn library. First, the LR and SVR object were created and called for the fit method to train the model for both by providing training datasets. Then, using objects called for the predicted method to generate predicted value for the testing dataset to test the models.

The performance is calculated using mean square error. Table 1 describes the details of the mean square error for both models for the Kharif and Rabi rice.

TABLE 2. Mean Square Error

Rice	Linear Regression MSR	Support Vector Regression MSR
Kharif	0.08740378578790721	0.0765240677533666
Rabi	0.1318635520786271	0.1328224734526147

CONCLUSION

In recent years a lot of attempts have been taken in the agro sector in various dimensions like IoT, Sensor, irrigation management, disease detection using image processing, yield prediction, etc. Many researchers have also implemented various machine learning techniques even hybrid to guide farmers and stakeholders in decision-making on agriculture management to improve food quality and quantity. In this research work, support vector regression and linear regression have been applied to predict rice yield prediction. It is observed that both are performing well in the dataset.

REFERENCES

[1]   H. Ait Issad, R. Aoudjit, and J. J. P. C. Rodrigues, "A comprehensive review of Data Mining techniques in smart agriculture," *Eng. Agric. Environ. Food*, vol. 12, no. 4, pp. 511–525, 2019, doi: 10.1016/j.eaef.2019.11.003.

[2]   "World population projected to reach 9.8 billion in 2050, and 11.2 billion in 2100," 2017. https://www.un.org/development/desa/en/news/population/world-population-prospects-2017.html.

[3]   "Machine Learning in Agriculture: Applications and Techniques," 2019. https://medium.com/sciforce/machine-learning-in-agriculture-applications-and-techniques-6ab501f4d1b5.

[4]   J. Behmann, A. K. Mahlein, T. Rumpf, C. Römer, and L. Plümer, "A review of advanced machine learning methods for the detection of biotic stress in precision crop protection," *Precis. Agric.*, vol. 16, no. 3, pp. 239–260, 2015, doi: 10.1007/s11119-014-9372-7.

[5]   A. Chakure, "Introduction to Machine Learning and Different types of Machine Learning Algorithms." https://hackernoon.com/introduction-to-machine-learning-and-different-types-of-machine-learning-algorithms-3z57i242u.

[6]   P. S. Maya Gopal and R. Bhargavi, "A novel approach for efficient crop yield prediction," *Comput. Electron. Agric.*, vol. 165, no. July, p. 104968, 2019, doi: 10.1016/j.compag.2019.104968.

[7]   P. Anitha and T. Chakravarthy, "Agricultural Crop Yield Prediction using Artificial Neural Network with Feed Forward Algorithm," *Int. J. Comput. Sci. Eng.*, vol. 6, no. 11, pp. 178–181, 2018, doi: 10.26438/ijcse/v6i11.178181.

[8]   N. Gandhi, O. Petkar, L. J. Armstrong, and A. K. Tripathy, "Rice crop yield prediction in India using support vector machines," *2016 13th Int. Jt. Conf. Comput. Sci. Softw. Eng. JCSSE 2016*, no. 2010, pp. 11–15, 2016, doi: 10.1109/JCSSE.2016.7748856.

[9]   H. Wang and Z. Ma, "Prediction of wheat stripe rust based on support vector machine," *Proc. - 2011 7th Int. Conf. Nat. Comput. ICNC 2011*, vol. 1, pp. 378–382, 2011, doi: 10.1109/ICNC.2011.6022095.

[10]   B. S. Anami, N. N. Malvade, and S. Palaiah, "Classification of yield affecting biotic and abiotic paddy crop stresses using field images," *Inf. Process. Agric.*, vol. 7, no. 2, pp. 272–285, 2020, doi: 10.1016/j.inpa.2019.08.005.

[11]   A. Gonzalez-Sanchez, J. Frausto-Solis, and W. Ojeda-Bustamante, "Predictive ability of machine learning methods for massive crop yield prediction," *Spanish J. Agric. Res.*, vol. 12, no. 2, pp. 313–328, 2014, doi: 10.5424/sjar/2014122-4439.

[12]   R. Grimm, T. Behrens, M. Märker, and H. Elsenbeer, "Soil organic carbon concentrations and stocks on Barro Colorado Island - Digital soil mapping using Random Forests analysis," *Geoderma*, vol. 146, no. 1–2, pp. 102–113, 2008, doi: 10.1016/j.geoderma.2008.05.008.

[13]   Z. Bo, S. ZhengHe, M. WenHua, M. EnRong, and Z. XiaoChao, "Agriculture extra-green image segmentation based on particle swarm optimization and k-means clustering.," *Nongye Jixie Xuebao = Trans. Chinese Soc. Agric.*, vol. 40, no. 8, pp. 166–169, 2009.

[14]   T. Xie, Z. Huang, Z. Chi, and T. Zhu, "Minimizing amortized cost of the on-demand irrigation system in smart farms," *Proc. - 2017 3rd Int. Work. Cyber-Physical Syst. Smart Water Networks, CySWATER 2017*, pp. 43–46, 2017, doi: 10.1145/3055366.3055370.

[15]   B. Ji, Y. Sun, S. Yang, and J. Wan, "Artificial neural networks for rice yield prediction in mountainous regions," *J. Agric. Sci.*, vol. 145, no. 3, pp. 249–261, 2007, doi: 10.1017/S0021859606006691.

[16] S. Veenadhari, D. Bharat Mishra, and D. C. Singh, "Soybean Productivity Modelling using Decision Tree Algorithms," *Int. J. Comput. Appl.*, vol. 27, no. 7, pp. 11–15, 2011, doi: 10.5120/3314-4549.

[17] S. Khaki and L. Wang, "Crop yield prediction using deep neural networks," *Front. Plant Sci.*, 2019, doi: 10.3389/fpls.2019.00621.